ANGELS FOUR

ANGELS

FOUR

by DAVID
NOTT

PRENTICE-HALL, INC.
Englewood Cliffs, N.J.

Designed by Linda Huber

ANGELS FOUR by David Nott

Printed in the United States of America • 3
Full-color insert printed in Japan.

Prentice-Hall International, Inc., London
Prentice-Hall of Australia, Pty. Ltd., North Sydney
Prentice-Hall of Canada, Ltd., Toronto
Prentice-Hall of India Private Ltd., New Delhi
Prentice-Hall of Japan, Inc., Tokyo

Library of Congress Cataloging in Publication Data
Nott, David.
    Angels four.
    Autobiographical.
    1. Angel Falls, Venezuela. I. Title
F2331.B6N6   918.7'6 [B]   70-180549
ISBN 0-13-036798-2

To Mariela

Acknowledgment

Thanks are due to Joseph Jesensky, who put his extensive file on the Auyán-Tepuí at our expedition's disposal, and furnished his maps of the region and his drawings of the mountain for this book; to Charles Burns, an adventurous soul himself, who dropped his professional commitments to provide the illustrations; to Father Carvajal and his staff at the Camarata Mission for their many kindnesses; to the Grupo de Rescate de Venezuela, which helped us obtain maps of the southern jungles and our permits to fly into them; and finally to the Venezuelan authorities who allowed us to reach and climb their country's greatest natural wonder, Angel Falls.

CONTENTS

INDIANS
AND CLIMBERS

O N E The Indians filed one by one into the patio of the mission building and I stood up to greet them. Father Carvajal, in his brown Capuchin robe, was working at a table a few feet away, rustling his papers. The Indians stood silently in the lantern light. They were Camaracotos and this was their village, Camarata, a scrubby little hamlet of forty families in the Gran Sabana of Venezuela.

"Buenas noches, señores," I said.

One or two nodded but none replied.

A young man came forward. He was barefoot, dressed in khaki slacks and a patched shirt. Under his stained felt jungle hat his hair was jet black, his face mahogany. *"Yo soy Alonso,"* he told me.

We sat facing each other on two chairs while I explained our plans.

"Alonso, we are going to climb the wall of the Angel Falls. You understand? *Escalar la pared del salto.* There are four of us and we want you to take us there and wait at base camp on the river for five days until we come down, and then bring us back here. Okay? *Está bien?*"

"Quieren ver el salto? You want to see the falls, señor?"

"Not see it. Climb it."

He stared at me somberly and shifted slightly on his chair.

"*En solo tres días* . . . in just three days I take you to the river camp. Next day you see falls and then down for sleep. Then we start back. *Está bien?* "

"No, no, Alonso. Listen carefully. We are going to *climb* the falls." I walked my fingers up the air in front of him. "Climb it to the top and then come down again. . . ."

I trailed off as Alonso glanced back at his companions. He seemed relieved to find they were still there, that he was not alone with this mad white man. "*No entiendo,*" he said.

Father Carvajal chuckled: "Señor Nott, I don't understand either. If you are hardy men, you make the journey to see the falls. You take a picture and you come back. The rapids and the jungle are enough adventure."

"No, padre. We're going up that damn . . . sorry, that blankety wall. Now which one can I talk to now? "

"They all want to talk to you. This is a rare chance for business. Let me remind you, our airstrip is our only contact with the outside world. There is no road. We don't often see . . ."

Another Indian had already stepped forward and sat down. He looked alert and intelligent. "Señor. I have a thirty-foot *curiara* and a twenty-horsepower outboard. You need that to get up the Churún rapids. I take you."

His businesslike approach surprised me. Studying him, I realized he had been with us from the minute we had landed in near darkness at the mission airstrip an hour ago. Our doctor and pilot, Paul Straub, had heard him say something in English and in his friendly way had greeted him like an old buddy. The Indian had latched on to him and put out feelers for a lift to Caracas or for cigarettes or unwanted equipment. I had sensed one of those have-not characters who demand the world from you unblushingly, with no gratitude if you come across and shrill insults if you don't.

I didn't like him, but he was direct and I responded in kind: "How much? "

"The price for two travelers up to the falls and back is 1,500 bolivars or $333. You are four, so the price is $666. But you want extra time too, so I charge extra for that."

I glanced at Father Carvajal but he was staring with undue interest at his sandals. I turned back to the Indian. I was beginning to like him even less.

"Look, hombre. So there are four of us. But we take our own food. We don't need extra crew. It's the same *curiara*. I think we should pay something more, but not double."

"You pay double, señor."

I watched the big jungle moths thumping against the lantern and tried another tack. "For your price I can get two *curiaras*, two outboards and two crews. For 1,500 bolivars each."

The man paused a moment, then leaned forward and spoke with an intensity that was odd in an Indian: "The truth, señor, is that that price is not realistic."

"It's not *what*? " I said, astonished and suddenly attentive to his tone.

Now what the hell have I got here? I won-

15

dered. Maybe I've misread this one. Maybe he's not a backwoods bandit but a genuine vanguard type who sees the price could be raised if he and his brother Indians were bold enough to do it. Perhaps he's just trying to set the pace for them even if he risks losing the job. This is just the sort of man to start the first Amerindian trade union, by God, and I like that. . . .

But we couldn't afford a dawning union movement in our dugout. There would be no room for pickets. I stood up and shook his hand with more than a slight feeling of capitalistic guilt. "Sorry, amigo. We don't have that much money."

Next a stocky young fellow approached, so cheerful and *simpático* I suspected he'd had a wee dram or two. I took to him immediately.

"*Mucho gusto, señor*," he said. "I am very happy to see you."

"Well, that's nice, old friend. What have *you* got? "

"Nothing," the Indian said. "But I have a brother with a big boat. Thirty-five feet long. Twenty-horsepower motor."

"Great. How much? "

"Feefty dollars."

I was sure about that dram now and, laughing, I pulled him to his feet.

"Hombre. You should join the union. For feefty dollars your brother wouldn't even let us *see* his boat."

A slight nod from Father Carvajal told me the next man was well thought of at the mission. He seemed about forty-five, and when he sat down before me he held himself aloofly erect. I was impressed. The man's name was Gabriel González. "We are going to climb straight up the wall of the falls, Gabriel."

I paused for a response. Gabriel stared back gravely without a flicker of expression. This is a gentleman of the old school, I told myself. With the manners of a grandee. He wouldn't ruffle his dignity or offend mine even if he thought I was plumb crazy. Hopefully I outlined our plans. "At the very most we will need you for eleven days. Perhaps two or three days to the falls and the same back. But we want you to wait for us for five days while we climb the wall."

I thought I was being persuasive and clear. Gabriel said nothing.

"Even if you can cut down the time we spend traveling," I said, "we'll pay you for the full eleven days."

Gabriel was immovable in his dignity. I looked at him closely and it dawned on me that his stare was not proud but plain glassy. I leaned forward. Gabriel smelled like a rum bottle. He was drunk. Magisterial but speechless.

"Well, I'll be damned," I said admiringly. "You could fool a policeman. We'll fix the price tomorrow. Be ready to go by noon."

I

DEVIL OR ANGEL?

The Auyán-Tepuí is a 250-square-mile plateau in the Guyana jungles of southeastern Venezuela, a remote, barely accessible region inhabited chiefly by Indians. Some 500 miles from the capital, Caracas, this area, with its dense green forests and winding rivers, is still not fully explored. Rising sheerly to a high point of 8,200 feet, shrouded for months at a time by clouds within which tropical storms flash and rumble, the plateau is a geographical monster, awesome and inhospitable. Some indication of how fearsome it is is given by its name. In the language of the Indians, "Auyán-Tepuí" means *Devil Mountain.*

The plateau is the most famous of the South American tabletop mountains which inspired Sir Arthur Conan Doyle's classic adventure novel, *The Lost World.* In this far-fetched romance (with melodramatic chapter headings such as "It Was Dreadful in the Forest" and "Our Eyes Have Seen Great Wonders") four Englishmen make their way to the top of a mysterious plateau where they find a prehistoric world of cavemen, dinosaurs, pterodactyls, even a freshwater plesiosaurus. The real "Lost World" of the Auyán-Tepuí does indeed abound in plants that exist nowhere else in the world. But there are no dinosaurs, only mosquitoes, lice, ants; all the myriad insects of the tropics.

What the plateau lacks in exotic beasts it makes up for with a more enduring wonder. A great gorge cuts into it from the north and down its western wall a river plunges in one swoop for 3,282 feet. This is Angel Falls, the highest waterfall in the world.

From a distance it looks like the towering exhaust trail of a moon rocket, from the churning clouds of vapor at its base to its narrow, stark-white apex. Close up it makes the same bellowing roar as the rocket blasting off. Twenty times higher than Niagara, its water takes fourteen seconds to reach bottom, nearly a quarter of a minute falling through space. Thousands of tons of it never reach the bottom at all except as fine, feathery mist.

That the most remarkable feature of Devil Mountain should bear the name of Angel is an irony for mystics to ponder. But there is no irony behind its dubbing, only simple fact. In 1935 an American pilot and soldier of fortune, looking for gold and diamonds, crash-landed his crimson-colored Cessna monoplane on top of the plateau; he escaped from the mountain after a three-week march southward to where the wall crumbles into a slope. His name was Jimmy Angel. He had known of the falls since 1923, having sighted it on one of his prospecting trips. Before then the earliest recorded report of its existence was as late as 1910, when the Venezuelan explorer Ernesto Sánchez La Cruz wrote that he had seen a river "that seemed to fall from the sky."

Since 1935 a number of expeditions have made the two-week march over gradually rising slopes from the south or west onto the plateau. Most of these were simply groups of adventurous souls who wanted an exciting trek and chose Angel's wrecked plane as the objective. The first expedition to reach the brink of the falls was in August, 1968, sponsored by the Explorer's Club and the Zoological Society, both of Pittsburgh, Pennsylvania, and by the Venezuelan Air Force. Before our own expedition, however, only two attempts had been made to climb the mammoth red and yellow sandstone walls that comprised the face of Angel Falls, and both had failed.

John Timo had been on both these attempts. He was a young medical X-ray technician from Bentleyville, Pennsylvania, a mountain climber, and had been a member of the climbing team attached to the 1968 expedition. The team had reached only 800 feet in three days when its food ran out and it was forced to retreat. In January, 1969, Timo was back as a member of another team, and this time they got to within a mere 500 feet of their goal before being defeated by unclimbable rock and a lack of water. The idea of climbing the wall had been his in the first place and it was an idea two defeats could not erase.

I had never met Timo before, so his invitation for me to join a third attempt came as a complete surprise. I was in my living room in Caracas one night in late December, 1970, with a scotch in hand, in training for Christmas, when he called me from Pittsburgh. He and two other men were flying down in a single-engine plane and planned to be on the wall within ten days. He had heard about my Andes expeditions from a Venezuelan friend and figured I might make a good fourth man. I was a climber but unfit. I was a trekker but had trekked nowhere for four months. I was forty-two and smoking like a chimney. But this was not the sort of invitation you turn down.

I hung up, went into the kitchen, poured my scotch down the sink and turned to my wife.

"Mariela. You're not going to like this. . . ."

II

SOMETHING WAY OUT

A few days later I was at Maiquetía International Airport and saw the winglights of their small plane dipping and banking in the dusk as it swooped down onto the runway, puny among the jets looming around it. It was a Mooney, number 7121 U, and I understood it belonged to one of our party, Paul Straub.

"Where the hell did that come from? " asked someone.

"Pittsburgh," I said as casually as I knew how. "Two thousand eight hundred miles away."

My fellow climbers had taken off from Pennsylvania's Allegheny County Airport on December 26, slept under the wings in overnight stops at Fort Lauderdale, Florida, and St. Croix in the U.S. Virgin Islands and crossed the Caribbean Sea to arrive in Venezuela on December 28.

The Mooney taxied up to its berth and I walked over to it with something more than curiosity. I had never met these three before and a difficult climb is not the best way to make friends. Of the four of us I would be the oldest and, as a transplanted Welshman, the only non-American.

The tiny door opened and the first man to duck out onto the wing was Timo. He was tall and lean and reserved in manner, almost grave. But I would learn later that this solemnity was due less to temperament than to the pressures he was under.

Despite the opinion of expert climbers who

21

said it was impossible, Timo was making his third attempt to climb the face of the falls and this time he was the leader. He was twenty-eight and two men in his team were ten and fourteen years his senior. From the start he used the word "gentlemen" whenever he addressed us as a group, an engaging mannerism that sidetracked his doubts about calling us "you guys."

The next to emerge was a dangerous-looking hombre with down-curving Mexican mustachios and a completely shaved head. He was a big fellow, twenty-six years old, and his name was George Bogel. As we shook hands he gave me a bandido's grin.

Third and last was Straub, the pilot. At thirty-eight Straub was closer to my own age but in superb condition, a strapping athlete with a surprisingly simple, gentle manner.

As we drove the twelve miles from the airport to Caracas we weighed each other up and I took the chance to broach two matters—my leg and the Palsy—which had been bothering me. I had had a parachuting accident the year before and had suffered three fractures in my left leg. There were still two screws in the bones and from time to time the leg would seize up. I really couldn't keep silent about it.

"John, there's something you ought to know. . . ."

"What's that, Dave?" asked Timo.

"I have a gammy leg."

"Excuse me?"

"He means a bum leg," translated Bogel, grinning. "These limeys think they speak English."

I explained the problem.

22

"Forget it, Dave," said Straub, the doctor. "I had the same fractures four years ago and still have one screw in. We're reinforced. It's *these* guys we have to worry about."

That left the Alpine Palsy, as I called it. Four months earlier I had been climbing in the Alps and had experienced repeated cramps in my arms on tough obstacles such as overhanging rock or steep ice. I had fallen several times but had been held by the rope and had escaped with no more than bruises. I had worked it out in my mind that if the Palsy recurred on the Angel it would be on the first day, allowing me to rope down without hindering the others.

"When it happens my hands just open up," I told Timo, "and I fall off."

"Hell," said Bogel. "We're a bunch of god-damn cripples."

We all laughed at that, but the punchline was still to come. Straub leaned over and tapped me on the shoulder.

"Listen, Dave," he said. "You think you've got problems. Here's something way out."

"What's that? " I said.

"I've never even climbed before," he said.

CHANCES
OF SURVIVAL

T W O Paul Straub was thirty-eight years old and a surgeon, practicing in New York City. He was also a pilot, which is why he had been asked to join our expedition in spite of the fact he had never climbed. Angel Falls is so remote, so cut off from civilization, that merely getting to it, let alone climbing it, poses a problem. For this, Straub and his Mooney had been enlisted. Since he was a rugged adventurous fellow, he had insisted in return on being included in the climbing team.

Six years before our climb, Straub had met a remarkable girl named Marjorie. Marjorie was thirteen years younger than he, pretty enough to have been a model, bright and a daredevil like himself. As Straub was fond of putting it, she was his "buddy." He'd go hunting, she'd go too. Parachuting, scuba diving, skiing, even drinking with the boys. She was his girl and his best friend, and Straub knew he was a lucky man.

He had always been a rolling stone, bumming around Europe and North Africa, gold prospecting in California. Part of the attraction of a medical career was that it could take him anywhere in the world. When he married Marjorie, a year and a half after meeting her, he rearranged his life radically, and happily.

He made the decision, not insignificant for a doctor, to specialize. This meant years more work and study before he would become the top ear, nose and throat surgeon he is today. He arranged to practice in Johnston, Pennsylvania, his home town and a far cry from the exotic ports he had once frequented. He wanted to give Marjorie a good life. They would make a home in Johnston, work a few years, then go off on safari or fly their tiny single-engined plane around the world.

Flying was Straub's favorite sport. He was a natural pilot and taught himself advanced aerial acrobatics before he even got his license. But even when he was performing stunts he was a meticulous aviator who regarded irresponsible flying as criminal.

Marjorie also flew. In fact she surpassed him at it. After Straub had taught her how to fly she went on to get a commercial pilot's and a flight instructor's license. She was twenty-three. It was the kind of thing that made Straub proud of his "buddy." While he worked and studied at his hospital, Marjorie taught at a flying school. Life seemed perfect.

Then, nine months before Straub was to finish his residency, the flight school telephoned him one afternoon. Marjorie had taken a pupil up and crashed. She was dead. That was in August, just four months before our expedition. Straub told me of his loss hesitantly, in bits and pieces, while we were traveling upriver and during our climb. It was clear he felt it deeply.

Three days before Marjorie's death she had written in the flyleaf of a book: "Life is no brief candle to me. It is a sort of splendid torch which I have got hold of for the moment, and I want to make it burn as brightly as possible before fate hands it on to future generations."

I

UNDER A JINX

If there was one thing our expedition had in abundance, it was bad luck. It showed itself at its most malignant in the incessantly rough weather, totally out of season, that we were to encounter on the climb.

But even before that, even before we reached the mission at Camarata, we ran into a series of setbacks and emergencies that had me thinking we were under a jinx. The fact that our funds, and especially our time, were limited, only increased our bondage to Dame Fortune.

The first setback involved our special dehydrated rations. They had not arrived from New York. These rations could not be bought in Venezuela and it would be impossible to haul ordinary supplies up the face of Angel Falls. We were between Christmas Day and New Year's Eve and could not expect the Chicago suppliers to pack and ship a new set in twenty-four hours.

Timo and I fell on the responsible airline like two scalded harpies. We browbeat the company Telex operator into sending an unauthorized message to New York in which we threatened legal action. We laid siege to the office and finally forced the manager himself to telephone the States.

"Listen," I told him, lying in my teeth. "All the international news agencies, two big television networks and three major magazines are covering this climb. The cameramen and reporters are arriving right now. They'll all get to Angel Falls and the ones who will be missing will be *us*. And why? Because *you* failed to deliver our rations. And that's exactly what we are going to tell them."

He made a soothing gesture with his hands but his eyes said: "Drop dead, you bastard."

Every wasted hour cut into our tight schedule. So next day Straub took off for Camarata with climbing kit, Bogel and Joseph Jesensky. He was to drop them at the mission and hightail it back to Caracas for Timo and me—and the rations. A 1,000-mile trip.

Jesensky was a sixty-five-year-old illustrator from Akron, Ohio, and one of the expedition's most important back-up men. Years ago Jesensky had developed a fascination for waterfalls. Any waterfalls, anywhere. One day he came across descriptions of the Auyán-Tepuí and Angel Falls and knew he had found a major interest of his life. He collected one of the largest set of records on the mountain that exists—films, recordings, pictures, maps, letters. All this he put at Timo's disposal. But for all these years Jesensky had never been to South America let alone the regions of the Lost World tablelands.

Now he had flown down from the States to

help. Timo was determined he should get at least a glimpse of the falls.

Late afternoon on the last day of the year saw Timo and me waiting despondently in my apartment. Then came two telephone calls in four minutes. First, Straub was back and standing by at Maiquetía. Second, the rations were in customs. We shot down to the airport, wheedled the crate out of a sympathetic official, slung it in back of the Mooney's cabin and were off, up and away eastward along the coast and then swinging southeast for the 350-mile flight to Ciudad Bolívar on the Orinoco River.

We had our permits for travel to the interior and we had left the capital behind. No more forms to fill, no more telephone calls, no more checklists. We crowed with delight in the cramped cabin. On our way at last!

But we had failed to reckon with the jinx.

II

LOSING OIL

Ciudad Bolívar, our first stop, is a town of 100,000 people and the gateway to the vast southeastern jungles of Venezuela. South of it is nothing but tiny settlements and Indian villages, and the forest sweeps on for hundreds of miles into the northern tip of Brazil. Its airport was the last on our route with illumination for night landings and radio beams for direction.

The Camarata airstrip, which would be our

destination the next day, had no lights or radio. A hundred and seventy-five miles farther south, it was no more than a strip of dirt with the rocks removed and we would have to find our way to it by following the major ground features: the Caroní and Paragua rivers and the satellite plateaus ringing the Auyán-Tepuí. Above all, we would have to get there in daylight.

It was a superb night, lit by a bomber's moon. Up front, Straub flicked on a light occasionally and rustled around with his map. I could see Timo's head in front of me black against the stars.

I dozed and woke to hear Straub's high, soft voice talking over the plane's radio:

"Ciudad Bolívar, this is Mooney 7121 Uniform. Do you read me. Over."

Crackling static and then a tough-guy controller's voice:

"Okay. 21 Uniform. Go Ahead."

"7121 Uniform to Ciudad Bolívar tower. I am twenty-five miles out, level 8,500. Over."

"Okay, 21 Uniform. Maintain course and level 8,500."

And on we drifted, steady as a jet, above the gigantic gas flares of the Anaco oilfields and the few scattered lights on the surrounding plains. I dozed again and sat upright as we banked sharply left over the bright, bead-strung lights of the Angostura Bridge, which crosses the Orinoco. The tight turn continued. Then we lurched and leveled for the glide down to the airport.

"Come in on runway zero six."

"Roger. 7121 Uniform."

Around us red rockets fizzed up and exploded. It was New Year's Eve.

We taxied to the terminal building, deserted by now, pushed the plane onto the grass and set off to hunt down the 100-octane aviation fuel we needed to make Camarata in the morning.

This was Thursday, the last night of the year. The only person around was a dispatcher about to go home. He was lazily attentive, then told us with complete indifference that we might get some gasoline on Monday. It was all I could do to keep my hands off his throat. At length we decided there was nothing to be done at this late hour, so we walked a mile down the road to an isolated hotel.

This was one of those outpost hostelries in Venezuela that are invariably run by Portuguese immigrants. They had probably started with an ice-cream stand and built it up by hard work and thrift. We were the only customers in the restaurant and our lentil soup and what-have-you was punctuated by the maddening bangs of firecrackers slipped by children under the chair of grandma, seated at the corner of the bar, who smiled and nodded her approval of this exquisite fun. Suddenly Straub pushed his plate away and announced we had a serious problem.

By God, I thought, the bloody jinx again.

"It's the oil," he said. "I'm losing oil. Would you believe we lost five liters out of eight just in this flight from Caracas? More than half what the engine holds in two hours. I didn't want to tell you, but when we landed there was oil streaked along the fuselage as far as the tail. We

31

have to get it looked at tomorrow. We can't fly to Camarata in the morning."

"Get it looked at? " I said. "But it's New Year's Day tomorrow. A national holiday. Nobody works."

"We've *got* to find someone, Dave," said Timo. "We can't lose another day. We *have* to get to Camarata tomorrow."

Dejectedly we returned to the airport and, on an off chance, walked over to a lit hangar. Surprisingly a cheerful individual and his girl friend were there sitting on bits of fuselage. He listened to our woes and perked us up immediately. "No worry at all, hombre. I'll dig a mechanic out myself and bring him here at nine sharp in the morning. Don't preoccupy yourself, chico. If he doesn't come I'll come myself anyway."

His name was Antonio Ching—nickname Chino. And I didn't believe a word he said . . . until he roared up the next morning on a motorbike, exuberant as ever. By the time he got there we had already found a mechanic living near the airport. He was in bed after a long night but we ruthlessly dragged him out and back to his workshop near the runway. By 11:00 all oil traces were cleaned off, the engine had been run at full blast for twenty minutes and the fault had been tracked down. Oil was leaking from the forward portside cylinder through what seemed to be a broken gasket.

Chino and his fellow fitter Luis Cabrera shook their heads.

"*Ustedes salen en eso, y se matan,*" Chino said.

32

I translated: "You take off in this, and you're dead."

Straub thumped his fist on the cowling. "Well, tell them to tighten it. Just so we can get to Camarata and back. I'll get it fixed properly before leaving for the States."

Sure. They could do that, said Chino doubtfully, but they didn't have a torque wrench for that size bolt. "The only one in this town belongs to a fellow who has a helicopter and he . . ."

But I was already shoving him toward his motorbike and at 11:30 we were hammering on the man's door, pleading, cajoling, threatening. It was no good. He was too ill to get up, said his wife. Hangover, said Chino. Bloody jinx, I muttered.

Back at the airport we watched tensely while our two mechanics manufactured a wrench with an iron rod, a nut and a soldering jet. They cooled it patiently, but with the first pressure on the cylinder bolt it broke. I propelled Chino back to his motorbike and in minutes I was on my knees before the sick man's wife.

"Please, señora, get the keys to the workshop and let's go get that wrench. Save the expedition and we will bless you for all time."

We followed the señora's red Mercedes Benz and rushed into the workshop excitedly, rummaging in the tool drawers, on the shelves and benches . . . and the bloody wrench wasn't there.

Back to the house. Husband relayed a message that so-and-so Sánchez had it and Chino, now in

33

a tizzy himself, drove like a lunatic through the mango-shaded streets, scattering groups of lovely Spanish-mulatto-Indian girls in their minis. We skidded to a stop at a house on a dirt road way out of town.

Sánchez didn't have it. He didn't even know where it was.

Back at the airport we howled against fate. For one lousy spanner the whole expedition was going off the rails. Timo looked thoughtful. "I have a feeling we're going to have a hard time on this trek." he said.

By 4 P.M. Luis and Chino had manufactured another wrench and we chewed our nails to the wrists as it cooled. We had to take off at 4:30 because nightfall was at six and we would never find the unlit Camarata airstrip in the dark.

The wrench worked! Ideally the job should have been done with a torque wrench tightening bolts in proper sequence around the cylinder but we settled for brute-force tightening of the only bolt we could reach without stripping off the exhausts.

At 4:40 we shot down the runway and up and away south, yelling and cheering but aware it was dangerously late. There were 175 miles of trackless jungle to cross.

III

RACE AGAINST DARKNESS

Within minutes we were flying over uninhabited terrain, a world of jungle and rivers. Straub handed me the map. "Check for airstrips," he said. "Maybe we could put down on one and top up with oil as the pressure falls."

As the pressure falls? My God! I thought it was fixed! And anyway there were no airstrips.

I sought out the oil gauge on the control panel and saw the needle flickering down into the yellow quadrant when it should have been well up into the green. I watched it in horrified fascination. If we didn't get to Camarata before dark we would never find the airstrip, and with pressure falling at that rate we would never make it back to Ciudad Bolívar.

Straub interrupted my calculations: "We'll cross to the Caroní River and follow it down to the falls at Canaima. Then we'll have to get across or around the Auyán-Tepuí fast and down to Camarata before dark."

Soon we were over the huge curves of the Caroní River and bore due south along them and checked the map as we crossed the Paragua River sweeping in a long golden curve from the south and west, only its surface lit by the sinking sun, the rest of the world in a monotone shadow.

"Well, we're okay for direction, fellows," said Straub. "All we need now is time."

Before long the mountains loomed up dramatically ahead and suddenly, out of the clouds tumbling and shifting about its summit, we spotted our target: the Auyán-Tepuí. It dwarfed everything around it. Canaima dropped behind to starboard and in the gathering darkness we climbed over the mountain's rim to take a line across it to the Acanán River. Somewhere along that line we knew we would pass over Angel

Falls but we didn't give it a second thought.
Night, oil and time filled our minds.

Now, surrounded by clouds, we were lost.
The terrain below—what we could see of it in
the gloom and the few gaps in the mist—was
savage. There were ridges and canyons, and rock
towers soaring out of dark ravines. One finger-
cluster of pinnacles, each of which we reckoned
to be 800 feet high, was just another feature in
this maze. Below us it grew blacker by the minute.

Straub spiraled the plane down a funnel in the
clouds. "Quick. Fix that river on the map," he
said. But the mist closed in and it was gone.

Then Timo and I were yelling in chorus:
"Look out! There's a cliff right ahead! In the
cloud! "

"Okay," said Straub. "I have it. Banking left
. . . Watch out, there's another one! Banking
right! Climbing! "

The engine roared as he gunned the plane
steeply upward. Even this high, as we leveled
off, the last glimmer of sunset had gone.

Abruptly we shot over the southwest edge of
the mountain, and Straub stood the plane on its
nose to dive straight down through the narrow
gap between the clouds and the wall to search
the valley in what was left of the light. My eyes
flicked to the oil gauge and back down to a river. The Acanán? A tributary?

Then Timo's voice, calm but an octave lower
than normal: "I think we should go right."

It was the last decision we had time for.
Down we went, following the river, until in the
last light, up ahead, we glimpsed a building. It

was the mission. In minutes we were over it and Straub said crisply: "Okay. Seat belts. We're going straight in."

A steep turn dragged my stomach into my boots. Straub eased the plane onto a dirt strip that I'll swear sloped upward into the darkness. We were in Camarata. And not a moment too soon, for the stars were already appearing.

IV

"YOU BREAK A LEG..."

It was nine o'clock now. I had finished interviewing the Indians and joined the others to help make up our packs.

This job had to be done with strict observance to weight. We were aiming for a maximum of seventy-five pounds per man, no mean burden to haul up 3,000 feet.

I remembered Eric Shipton, the great Himalayan explorer for whom I had worked years ago as an instructor at a British Outward Bound Mountain School. Shipton was the sort who would start a three-month expedition with only a single shirt, and I found my companions had similar notions. Each had a parka, a shirt and a pair of pants. Straub and Bogel had a sleeping bag each and a waterproof sheet for cover. Timo had a jungle hammock that was waterproof top and bottom. In this he wrapped what I think he called his thermal underwear, I never could get the word straight—thermos, thermonuclear, thermo something. Anyway, they were longjohns with a long-sleeved top and were meant to keep him warm at night.

My scheme for the cold, wet nights was an extra waterproof parka and a plastic garbage bag that came up to my armpits. No sleeping bag or groundsheet. With this outfit I reckoned I could sleep in the rain without cover and keep warm. I couldn't have been more mistaken.

This was fairly Spartan gear, I thought, and nobody could fault us on the score of sissified clothing. But I felt skeptical about the cooking kit. We each had a small mess-tin for eating. Then there were two half-gallon pots, a big Teflon frying pan and two small butane camping stoves with half-a-dozen spare cartridges. I thought we might be overdoing it and opened my campaign with another tale about Shipton.

This hard-traveling man came through Venezuela in 1962 on his way to cross the formidable ice-cap in Patagonia. He, George Band of Everest and Kanchenjunga fame and I guided a party of Dutch oilmen who had never before climbed up the 16,000-foot Pico Bolívar in one day in terrible weather. For my rations I took one can of beans. In the plane on the way back to Caracas, Shipton asked me what I had done with the beans and I told him I had eaten them . . . with a piton.

"You don't heat these things? "

"No. I eat anything, cooked or uncooked."

Shipton, an admirably reserved man, was silent for about five minutes. Then he turned to me: "Would you like to come to Patagonia?..."

Timo laughed but went on stacking up the pans. I tried another tack. In Britain, I said, climbers eat what they call a "hoosh." You carry only one pot, fill it with water and sling everything you have into it. It's great stuff, fellows. You all eat from the same pot, then you make your tea in it. No washing, no weight.

Timo nodded: "But I'm interested in the team's health, not typhoid. Food has to be attractive. It will be tough enough up there and we have to eat."

I saw tins of nuts and Spam, chocolate bars and cookies going into the bag and I started snorting.

"We'll be glad of these little extras up on the wall, Dave, and they only weigh five pounds," Timo said.

Our dehydrated rations (donated by Bernard Food Industries Inc., of Chicago) were powders in aluminum foil, paper-covered packets. You empty the powder into water and heat it or not according to what you're mixing. They have marvelous American names. One is called Instant Zoom Cereal Mix.

"I say, Paul. Would you pass me the Instant Zoom Cereal Mix?" What it is, of course, is porridge.

We finally got the essential kit into four rucksacks and one duffelbag. We would each be carrying a small climbing pack as well. The food, enough for four men for ten days, weighed seventy-five pounds. Cooking and personal gear, sixty pounds. Climbing kit, including three ropes 120, 150 and 200 feet long, amounted to seventy-five pounds. Bogel had brought two cliff-hangers, which are small steel hooks you can hang on tiny wrinkles in tight situations. He had one rurp—Realized Ultimate Reality Piton, a minuscule shred of metal you hammer into tiny cracks and tie onto. We also had a set of bolts that you drive into the rock when not even faith remains. They are despised by purists.

The weight of all this, 210 pounds, would be increased by ninety pounds when we filled our two five-gallon plastic water containers at the base of the falls. The total, 300 pounds, fitted our estimate exactly.

One of the smallest items among the equipment was Straub's medical bag, a reminder of how little could be done for any one of us who fell. On the face of Angel Falls there was no hope of rescue. In the Alps a strong team of guides can bring an injured climber down from almost any situation. But in Venezuela there are no guides; around the Auyán-Tepuí north wall there aren't even any people. We would have to rely on ourselves.

But even if three men could get an injured companion off the wall it would take them at least two days to get him down to the Churún River, the nearest point the *curiaras* could reach. Then there would be the rapids to run and the long pull up the Carrao and Acanán rivers, before reaching the Camarata mission. With a disabled man, this could take four days. How long it would take to get him down the wall in the first place could not be calculated. It would depend on how high up the accident occurred. And if the injury was serious it would be impossible anyway.

I hefted the little medical bag in my hand. "So that's our field hospital."

"That's it, Dave," said Bogel. "You break a leg and you're dead."

THREE

JOURNEY TO THE FALLS

We left Camarata at two o'clock in the afternoon. In the morning Straub had topped up his engine with oil and flown Timo, Bogel and Jesensky to the Auyán-Tepuí and as close to the falls as the clouds would permit.

Timo knew the route as far as the high point of the 1969 expedition. But there was a danger that above the high point it would lead us not to the summit but to the top of a pinnacle detached from the main face. This had to be checked. But for all Straub's skill Timo and Bogel got no clear view of the upper face through the mist. Jesensky, however, had seen the falls at last.

They flew on to Canaima thirty miles northwest of the falls, where there was a dirt airstrip and a tourist lodge. The Radio Caracas Televisión station had hired a small plane to film our ascent and this was to be its base. Jesensky would stay there as liaison man and we would carry a small receiver-transmitter on the climb as radio link with the pilot. Jesensky installed and radio signals arranged, Straub topped up with oil again and flew back to Camarata with Timo and Bogel.

43

While they were away Gabriel, sober but no less dignified, had come to the mission to settle the price. We agreed on 2,440 bolivars, or $542. I gave him 1,000 bolivars on the spot, the rest to be paid on our return. When the others got back, Straub accepted the price instantly and Timo did so after a few minutes' thought. Bogel blew his top.

"How the hell did the price get up there?" he fumed. He was convinced I had taken the first figure Gabriel had thrown at me. "A day's pay for an Indian is 20 bolivars! How many weeks are we supposed to be on the damn river?"

But Bogel was like a tropical thunderstorm. He rumbled and roared and was immediately sunshine again, grinning beneath his bandit's mustache. We hustled him out to the jeep, loaded the kit and drove down to the river.

Father Carvajal still had his doubts about our project.

"Do you have any children, Señor Nott? " he asked me as we stood on the bank.

"Yes," I said. "Four. Dominique, Vivian, Millicent and David."

"They are your four best reasons for not climbing that wall."

"Not *that* gang, Father. They'll disown me if I don't make it."

He was still shaking his head when we finished loading the *curiara* and, with a final wave to him, shoved off down the Acanán.

JUNGLE RIVERS

Our sixty-mile journey to the falls would follow stretches of four rivers, the Acanán, the Carrao, the Churún and the Angel. The first three we would cover by *curiara* and the last on foot. The rivers would take us in a long curve around the north end of the mountain and south into the Churún Gorge, which cuts into it. The Angel River starts on top of the Auyán-Tepuí plateau, drops over the edge to form the falls, then continues down from the bottom to meet the Churún. This junction would be the site of our base camp. The time this journey takes depends on the season and the depth of water in the rivers, especially in the Churún, which has long stretches of rapids. We started from Camarata at two o'clock on Saturday afternoon and reached base camp midmorning on Monday, a relatively fast time.

The *curiara* is an authentic native craft burned and hollowed out of single log. Ours was four feet wide at the center and thirty feet long. It had taken Gabriel a full year to make. Its equipment consisted of two four-foot paddles and two long poles cut from saplings. The outboard motor on the stern was a modern addition and one that looked suspiciously small for the job. Gabriel assured us its nine-and-a-half horsepower would be enough to force up the Churún rapids. We were to discover it wasn't.

Just as our team was a mixture of types and personalities, so was the crew. Gabriel was the quiet, dignified captain. Miguel, his son, was twenty, keen to learn his trade on the river, and shy. Antonio Vargas, twenty-five years old, jungle hat tipped forward, cigarette in the corner of his mouth, was the cool cat. He never spoke. Finally there was Fabricio Vargas, the sea-lawyer, subjecting long-suffering Gabriel to a constant stream of unwanted instructions and advice. Fabricio was forty-two, exuberant and forever reminding me that a bottle of scotch would be well-received when the expedition was over. He worked as hard as he talked.

Fabricio took the lookout spot in the prow watching for logs and rocks. Behind him was Antonio. We four sat in the middle with a drum of gasoline before and a pile of gear behind. Miguel sat in front of his father, who handled the motor.

In the five-hour trip down the Acanán there are three sets of rapids, each dropping twenty feet in fifty yards. During rainy season when the water is deeper you can shoot these without stopping. But we had to go ashore above them and carry the packs around while Gabriel and crew wrestled the boat down and came inshore to pick us up. Between the rapids the going was smooth. From time to time we passed an Indian hut and at one where a mother was washing clothes in the river with a row of pretty children at her side, Straub said: "Say, that's nice. Marjorie would like that."

We lay back on the packs and watched the banks for jungle life. We had hoped for anacondas and crocodiles but all we saw was the odd turtle.

46

Birds, however, were more plentiful. There were pairs of brilliant red and green parakeets and in one high tree, an eagle, or at least a snooty-looking vulture. Then there were the herons. Dazzling white in the trees, they would take off as we approached and fly downriver, perch again and, as we drew near, take flight again, moving farther from their roosts each time. *"Están locos,"* said Fabricio. "They crazy." It was a game for the Indians to see how far the herons would go before it occurred to them that the only way to be rid of us was to double back over the boat.

II

SHOOTING AND PUNTING

Rounding a bend Gabriel gave a shout and pointed downstream: *"Mira, mira!"* A big bird was flying toward us, skimming the surface. Deftly Antonio slipped a single-barrel shotgun from under the gear and we sat up excitedly to enjoy some Indian marksmanship. Antonio watched the bird coming but coolly kept his gun across his knees. He's a crack shot, I thought. The bird drew level, Antonio flashed the gun to his shoulder and fired. The bird flew on without even ruffling its feathers.

We slumped back and Antonio reloaded. Within minutes Gabriel yelled again. *"Mira!* Look there!" Once more we sat up as a flock of pigeons flew toward us at treetop height, their wings flickering against the sky. The Indian fired and we could see the cluster of pellets against the blue, three yards behind the last bird.

We slumped back again, disappointed and surprised. Antonio was shooting to eat, not for sport. But not only did he apparently not know how to shoot his weapon, he did not know how to look after it either. The wooden stock was bleached and dry; it had not been oiled in years.

The Indians showed the same lack of skill with the poles. When running up a mild rapids where the boat could hold its own but not advance, one crewman in front and one in back would pole up until the current eased. But their technique was all wrong. Even the greenest Cambridge undergraduate does better punting his lady upriver. He flips the pole straight forward and up and pushes again in half the time it took our crew.

I mentioned this to the others and only Straub understood my reference.

"Punt? " Timo said.

"What's a punt? " asked Bogel.

I stared nonplussed at the doctor.

"Generation gap, Dave" he said.

III

GHOST TOWN

It took twenty-five minutes to get the boat down the third rapids and an hour later it was dark. I asked Gabriel where we would camp for the night.

"*En el pueblo fantasma*," he said with a half-smile. "In ghost town."

As we ran the boat ashore he told me the place was called Carrao, although that river was still four miles away. There was a deserted airstrip and the bones of a crashed DC-3. On each side of a rutted track were a dozen wood-pole skeletons of shacks with rags and tatters hanging from them of that paper-thin corrugated tin you can almost tear with your hands. It rustled and squeaked and made sad little tings in the wind. We probed around cautiously. In one ruin we found the remains of a large expensive electric fan, and in another, so help me, of a six-foot-tall jukebox, a rusty nickelodeon in a shanty with one tin wall and no roof.

Carrao had been a wham-bang diamond miners' stage-post, a place sourdoughs could reach in a day or two when they'd collected a packet of stones, or were so far gone out of their minds with shoveling and sieving that they had to have a beer and see another face. Now it was dead.

Suddenly I jerked around. A lantern flickered down the track. I sought out Gabriel among the huts. "Listen, hombre," I said. "There's one of your ghosts here walking around with a lamp."

"*Cómo?*"

"Look at that light," I said.

"Ah, sí. That's Señor Rogelio."

Señor Rogelio, I thought. Our Friendly Spook.

"Come. I introduce you," said Gabriel.

49

Señor Rogelio was a white man. He was wearing a sweatshirt with a paint manufacturer's slogan on it and a pair of those heavy-framed glasses businessmen think make them look tough. He was about fifty, short and tubby.

I shook his hand. "*Mucho gusto*," he said. "D'you need anything? Biscuits? Spam? Beer?"

"You have to be kidding, spook," I said in English.

"*Cómo?*"

"Beer, did you say? *Cerveza?*"

I raised my voice to a shout. "Paul! There's a guy down here with *beer!*"

Straub, Timo and Bogel came pounding down the track.

"What's going on?"

"Who said beer?"

Señor Rogelio crossed to a hut with four walls and a roof and unlocked the door. We filed in in the lantern-light. It was a general store and among the goods for sale were string, nails, candles, tin mugs, enamel plates, tinned food and, amazingly, ice-cold beer in a kerosene-powered deep-freeze.

"Well I'll be damned," said Straub. "Give us a couple of cans, will you?"

Bogel picked up a flower-decorated enamel mug and turned it over. "Hey, fellows. D'you know where this was made? Czechoslovakia!"

He eyed Señor Rogelio: "Maybe this guy's a Red agent."

When things calmed down a bit I talked to our storekeeper. No, he said, he was not lonely. He had his radio and the Indians passed down the river once in a while. They bought supplies

50

and chatted. I asked him how he had come to Carrao in the first place. He said that when news of a diamond strike reached Ciudad Bolívar prospectors had stampeded down here with pickaxes and bags of rice and beans.

"I waited a little. Then when I thought they'd be breaking tools and running out of supplies I turned up with ten-dozen picks and half a ton of tinned food. I was in business."

"And the good old days with the jukebox?" I said. "You didn't want to leave when it all folded?"

"No, amigo. I found I like isolation. I'm no pioneer, understand? I don't want to carve anything out of this jungle. I could be in the desert or the mountains. It's all the same. But I can't live in a town anymore."

We shook his hand approvingly and trooped off to make camp. Farther up the track we found the Indians in another hut boasting walls and a roof. It even had a concrete floor and seemed an obvious berth for the night.

IV

THE HARD-SLEEPING LIST

A crucial test for trekkers is how they sleep in rough conditions. This is particularly important for the climber who may find himself, as we would night after night, perched on tiny ledges or tied to spikes in the rock. In the ghost town we were to find out who was who on the hard-sleeping list.

The Indians had built a fire in the corner of the hut and strung up their hammocks from the support poles. Timo hung his among them and Straub laid out an air-mattress. Bogel unrolled his sleeping bag to lie on while I would use a pair of socks to go under my hip and boots to go under my head. We cooked by the light of candles bought from the store. But crouched over the camping stove, we failed to notice the smoke was thick under the roof and descending lower every minute. Standing up to get his pack, Timo, I swear, vanished in the cloud from the waist up. He sat down with his eyes watering.

"You'd better get your hammock down and sleep on the floor like the rest of us," I said.

"If the Indians can stand it, so can I," said he.

I asked Gabriel how he could sleep in the smoke.

"You have to," he said. "Otherwise the mosquitoes will eat you alive."

Timo climbed into his hammock and not another sound was heard from him for the rest of the night. Straub, the dude with the air-mattress, was asleep in minutes. Bogel stretched out contentedly on his sleeping bag and I on my socks and boots. Outside it was raining and inside the smoke crept lower until it was a foot from the floor.

Under it, all the mosquitoes in Carrao were concentrated, whining and shrilling about our ears, stinging and biting wherever they could get at our skin.

I was the first to cut and run. After an hour of acrid smoke, hard concrete and dive-bombing mosquitoes as big as birds, I crossed the tracks to a hut with a roof but no walls. Here I slung a pocket nylon hammock and climbed into it bent like a hairpin, legs in the garbage bag, hands under my armpits. Only my nose protruded from the hood of my parka and on it the bombers zeroed in as I swung miserably. Half an hour later Bogel shot out of the hut spluttering and cursing, got into his sleeping bag beneath me and zipped it up over his head. Another hour twisting in the hammock and I cut loose again. I stumbled up the track, flopped down on the dirt airstrip, felt around for a rock for a pillow and dozed fitfully in the rain until dawn. Straub slept the whole night without a twitch.

This set the pattern for the expedition. I was the alarm clock, the insomniac who shakes the others at the first glimmer of light and says it's late, time to be moving.

On the roughest nights on the wall not even Straub would be able to sleep for more than five minutes at a stretch.

V

OF WATER AND RAIN

Twenty minutes downstream next morning we reached the Carrao. It was a big, wide river and, except for two rapids, as placid as a pond. At last we could really see the "black waters" of the Gran Sabana. Whatever their mineral content, these rivers were black in deep water, blood-red close to shore and, if you scooped out a glassful, pale gold. Fabrico said it looked like champagne but he would settle for that bottle of whisky. With brilliant yellow and green mosses under the surface, the rivers were strangely beautiful. Strange because there was no blue in them even when the sky was cloudless. On the dark surface the reflection of the trees was immaculate.

We were about to get a closer look at this water. After six hours on the Carrao we turned left up the Churún and entered the rapids. My log read: "1320 hours, turned up Churún. 1400 hours, first rapids." It ended abruptly here and became a soggy wad of paper, for as I was scribbling Gabriel shouted: "*Fuera*! Everyone overboard!"

He switched off the motor and all eight of us jumped in, scrabbled for footholds on the boulders in the riverbed and began shoving the *curiara* slowly against the cold, fierce current. "*Uno, dos. Ya!*" Gabriel chanted. "One, two. Now!" And we heaved in rhythm. Every few minutes one of us would stumble and vanish beneath the surface.

It took twenty-five minutes to get through this first rapids, and once in calmer water we found we had the same fear in mind. The bottom was a dangerous jumble of boulders. If one of us sprained or broke an ankle the expedition would be finished. I explained the problem to Gabriel.

"I'm sorry, señores," he said. "There is more water than I expected. There must be heavy rain on the Auyán-Tepuí."

54

He had given us the first intimation of the weather that awaited us on the wall.

"Did you hear that, John?" I said.

"Yes. And I don't like it. When it rains up there you don't get just wet rock but rock with slime on it. It runs down from the vegetation on the ledges."

For a climber this would be like an oil slick on a corner for a racing driver. Timo had been through it. The wet season in the region is from April to October. The first attempt to climb the face of the falls had been in the month of August and was seriously handicapped by the persistent downpour and slippery rock. This is why the team had made only 800 feet in three days, an exceptionally slow rate for any climb. But with plastic sheets as rain-catchers they had had no lack of water.

The second attempt, on the other hand, had been at the height of the dry season in January, 1969. The rock was dry and the team climbed three times as far in the same number of days. But this time it had been forced down by thirst.

Since slimy rock was unquestionably the most dangerous factor, Timo had chosen the dry season again for this third attempt. As a result we would have to carry our own water, which would amount to ninety pounds extra weight. We were also bringing rain-catchers, just in case.

"We're going to get the worst of both worlds," I said. "If it's raining up there now, the rock will be as dangerous as in the wet season. But we'll still have to carry water because there's no guarantee there'll be rain to catch when we need it."

VI

A MATTER OF SCALE

The rapids continued intermittently for two hours and, ankles or no ankles, we heaved up them all. Then three hours before we ran the boat ashore for the night we came to a level stretch, rounded a bend and there before us was the Auyán-Tepuí, stretching for miles on either side, soaring 3,000 feet up from the jungle.

The mind slips gears trying to take in a colossus like this, especially when you encounter it unexpectedly. I recalled docking a ketch in a busy port months before and sleeping on board. In the morning there was a great freighter alongside. It had berthed in the night and now, at dawn, suddenly loomed immense above me. But compared with this wall ahead, the freighter seemed a toy. The Auyán-Tepuí was like a separate planet rearing over the rim of the world.

We began tracing routes up it, as climbers will. It was difficult to grasp the scale. I peered at a fissure in the face—a thin dark scar running up a third of its height—and realized with a jolt that you could tuck a hundred-story skyscraper into it. A smooth slab of rock above the fissure was as large as six football fields laid end to end in pairs, 900 feet high, 300 wide. And if we climbed that far we would still be a thousand feet from the top.

Studying the shadows I saw the football-field slab was separated from the face. It was a gigantic pinnacle. I pointed it out to Timo and he frowned.

"Dave, now you know the size of things around here. Ending up on a pinnacle like that is the worst single nightmare I have about this expedition. And by the lie of the rock on our route it's a real danger."

I looked back at the slab. If we ended on such a pinnacle it would be an absurd defeat. We might be almost as high as the top but it would not be the real top, and we had no rations for a second try on another route. Then and there we named a new phobia in our lives: "Pinnaclitis." It was to impel us into several dangerous maneuvers on the climb.

The falls and our point of attack were still miles to the south. But it was the same wall.

"So we're going to be four days and nights on that, John?" said Straub.

"I hope it's only four," said Timo.

It was going to be ten.

HOW TO LEARN
MOUNTAIN CLIMBING
THE HARD WAY

FOUR

Paul Straub had never climbed before, and now that we could see the great wall ahead, the implications seemed serious and immediate. Climbing is a demanding sport. Techniques vary from delicate-balance moves on friction holds to violent heaves over overhangs where you need a grip like a gorilla's. All the surfaces on a rock face—slabs, cracks, walls, chimneys—require different techniques, and these can be mastered only with experience. More important, you must be mentally prepared. In most games, if you make a wrong move you lose a point, a goal or a run. In climbing you can lose your life. Straub had no technique. Worse, he would begin his education not with a beginner's route on a practice cliff but with the immense unclimbed face of Angel Falls.

By the end of the second day's climbing, as if peeved with this temerity, the mountain was to literally take everything from him except the clothes he stood in. It would give him, in return, a harsh but thorough schooling.

I

WATER LOSS

After a couple of hours' run next morning we reached the junction of the Churún and Angel rivers. This was the site of base camp. We went ashore, stowed all nonessentials in a plastic bag, cached it and followed the three-mile jungle track, roughly parallel to the Angel River, toward the base of the falls. The trail ended on a lookout rock on the south bank of the river, and here the Indians left us to return to base camp to wait the four or five days we expected to be on the face.

Three-quarters of a mile dead-ahead and 300 feet higher was the bottom of the falls. We ran our eyes straight up maybe 2,000 feet, at which point the great gout of water vanished in the clouds. We were looking up the equivalent of two Empire State buildings one on top of the other and knew there was still a third on top of that before the rim of the mountain was reached. And where the Empire State is vertical, this wall was more so; it overhung in places for hundreds of feet at a stretch. Timo stared at it, totally expressionless. He had seen it twice before from this vantage.

"We've got to get it this time," he said.

We forced up through steep, dense jungle, crossed the rapids on the Angel River and climbed a stony slope 500 feet high to where the forest clustered at the foot of the wall. The slope was hard going, with scrub growing treacherously over the boulders, and it ended with a slimy forty-foot-high cleft in the rock. Here Timo skirted the wall to a point almost directly under the falls to fill the two water containers.

By the time we had all packs and water up the cleft it was dusk. We were on a narrow ridge in thick vegetation with a drop into gullies on either side. It had begun to rain while we were on the slope and we were in any case soaked from the sodden brush.

But much as we needed it, a full two hours' work in the windy darkness failed to produce even a halfway decent bivouac. We rigged a fly-sheet from the branches, had no success in getting a fire going under it and finally turned in, Bogel, Straub and I clinging to lumps in the rock to avoid rolling off the ridge, Timo as usual in his hammock, slung up somewhere in the swishing trees.

The heavy rain was discouraging. Every hour of it reduced our chances on the wall. But there was also temptation in it.

"If we could be sure it would rain like this every couple of days we wouldn't have to drag ninety pounds of water up the face," I said. "We have four plastic sheets for rain-catchers after all."

"We can't risk it," Bogel said. "The last expedition failed because it ran out of water. We've got to haul those tanks."

Timo's voice floated from above: "Believe me, gentlemen, nothing is more crucial to this expedition than those two water containers."

This sort of statement, we were to discover, was asking for trouble on the Angel. Packing up at dawn the next morning, Timo sorted the pro-

visions, Bogel, the climbing equipment, while
Straub and I dealt with the groundsheets and
cooking kit. As Timo dropped one of the water
containers at my feet to be put in the duffel, he
gave a shout.

We jerked around. "What's wrong?" said
Straub.

"We've lost half our water supply," Timo
said.

He was bent over the container and we saw a
two-inch gash at the top.

How it had happened was a mystery, but the
tank was useless. Counting our own water bottles we had eight gallons of water left: a quart a
day for each man for six days. But we needed
this for more than drinking; our food was dehydrated, so without water we couldn't eat either.
We would have to ration ourselves strictly, and
catching rainwater somewhere up the face had
now become vital.

II

BAPTISM OF FIRE

The day's objective was the first major ledge
of the wall, about 300 feet above. Even without
having to haul three heavy packs, the big duffel,
the spare rope, the water and three climbing
packs, it was some of the most difficult rock of
the whole route.

"We start some way along to the right," Timo
said. "We better divide the kit and get going."

Two Abject Beings, Nott and Straub, rest on a ledge waiting for supper. The author (left), cold but too tired to think, has put his shirt on over his parka.

Straub moves off the bivouac ledge above the Tyrolean Traverse to begin the last big vegetation pitch on the seventh day of climbing.

On the summit. Left to right: the author with Union Jack, Bogel with the pennant of the Explorer's Club of Pittsburgh, Timo with the Venezuelan flag, and Straub with Old Glory. The picture was taken with a timing device on the camera perched on a rock.

Straub about to step backward over the edge in a rappel on the descent. The jungle is 2,000 feet below. The river is the Churun. Bogel below.

The starting point was a ten-foot cleft with a fifteen-foot corner above it. The cleft began at the highest point of the jungle slope just before it dropped off to the north. This was it.

Normally in climbing, the best man goes first. He ties the rope around his waist and climbs until he reaches a safe belay point to which he can secure himself. The belay may be a spike of rock or a tree, and there should preferably be a little ledge, or stance, on which he can stand. The leader may climb thirty, fifty, or even 120 feet before he finds a belay. If he cannot find one at all he hammers a piton into a crack in the rock and uses that. Pitons are steel spikes of various shapes about four inches long. The stretch between belays is called a pitch. The leader ties himself to the belay and pulls the rope up until he feels the second climber on the other end. As the second man climbs, the leader takes in the slack. If the second man falls, the leader braces himself and holds him with the rope. If the leader is dragged off his stance by the fall, he is still attached to the belay and both men will hang from it until they can get back onto their holds.

It is far more dangerous when the leader falls. Suppose he has climbed sixty feet above the second man and slips. He will fall not only sixty feet to the level of the second man but another sixty feet before the rope stops him. The climber who slips 100 feet above his second man will fall 200 feet before the rope stops him—*if* it stops him. Not many ropes, or men, survive a fall of that height.

On more difficult routes the leader can protect himself with what are called running belays, which shorten his fall. They are rigged by hammering a piton in, clipping a karabiner—a four-inch metal snap-link—into it, and running the rope through it. But normally he relies on his skill and nerve, and this is what the game is all about. Climbing steep rock high above your second man is airy and exhilarating. Every move is a risk and one you must face on your own. As in sky-diving, skiing or motor racing, you must make your decisions by yourself—and they must be right. We had explained all this to Straub on the river, but it was a lot to swallow in one gulp.

Timo tied the rope around his waist and started up. We followed in turn, climbing and pack-hauling in quick succession. Then, traversing right, we found ourselves perched over a point where the jungle slope dropped away 200 feet. We were about to have our first real taste of Auyán-Tepuí climbing.

The obstacle was a vertical thirty-foot crack, smooth and slippery. It was just wide enough to jam in your left arm and shoulder and your knee and foot. There were only a few wrinkles for holds and the only way to scale it was to jam in your limbs, edge up and jam in again. For Straub, it was a baptism of fire.

He struggled a few feet, then fell, and I braced to hold him. He tried again and fell again. Tried and fell. I could hear his breath rasping as he strove now simply to stay in place.

"There's no holds. Just not any holds. How can I . . . ?"

"Jam, Paul. Jam your arms, feet, knees, anything. Wriggle up and jam again. Don't lose even

66

two inches you've gained or you'll never make it."

He climbed two or three feet and slipped again.

"Paul. Can you keep yourself in place just a second without the rope holding you?"

"I think so."

Quickly I hitched the rope over the remnant of an old tree above my head. It was about three inches thick. Now every inch Straub gained I consolidated by a turn of the rope around the tree. Slowly he struggled upward, six, ten, twelve feet. Suddenly the tree snapped off with a doomsday crack and Straub fell, yanking me headfirst off my stance. Almost immediately we were stopped by my rope, secured to the belay, and I hung head down for a second or two before Straub got back onto the rock and took his weight off me, then I scrambled back onto the stance.

We had been at it more than an hour and Timo came down to see what was keeping us.

"Paul's in trouble," I said. "He's too heavy for me to pull up."

Tying half-a-dozen loops in his rope for Straub to use as holds, Timo dropped it down to him. With this makeshift ladder and my protective rope the doctor came up quickly, soaked in sweat.

"Sorry, Dave," he gasped. "That must have been hard work holding me."

There was more of it to come. While Straub struggled through his harsh apprenticeship, I was always the man above, holding him when he fell. And he weighed 180 pounds to my 140. Farther up the wall, when the Palsy hit me, he would return the favor in full.

Next came an intricate series of cracks, slabs and traverses. At five o'clock we found ourselves and the packs crowded on a small ledge. Above us the face rose in jutting noses and overhangs. Timo leaned out and looked up.

"The next 100 feet are tough. I don't think we should try it. It's too late."

I glanced over the edge at the jungle below. We were only 150 feet up, a poor start on a climb of 3,000 feet. "So that's all we make in a whole day," I said.

"I'm afraid so. This ledge is as far as we go."

We studied it in disgust. It was only two feet wide and on it we must spend the night: our first bivouac on the wall.

Pulling ourselves together, we surveyed our aerie. There was a tree growing from a crack below, and with a few gymnastics we got enough wood to make a fire. The operation brought us fuel but it cost us our light. In the confusion someone kicked the bivouac lantern over the edge. Now the ledge took on the air of a confessional. With rising embarrassment we offered our contributions to replace it. Bogel nothing. Straub, nothing. Timo, who had brought the lantern, a two-dime plastic job that didn't work. Me, a penlight that was on the point of expiring and a scuba-diving lamp. But I had left the spare batteries in Caracas to save weight.

"So that's all we have," said Timo. "We should use it only in emergency. We'll have to do everything in the bivouacs by firelight. When we have a fire, that is."

68

Thus our caveman existence began. As night hid the drop beneath we cooked and ate, chattering like thieves in the flickering flames.

Timo hung his hammock in the tree with nothing between him and the jungle but air. The rest of us kicked the embers of the fire over the edge and squeezed down on the warm rock as best we could. All of us were tied to the tree in case we fell off while sleeping.

Sleeping? On a ledge like this? Straub was snoring within minutes. His head was on my hipbone, and whenever I turned it thudded into the pit of my stomach. I counted the hours as the night dragged by, cloudless at first and then with heavy rain. But the doctor slept through it all, warm and secure in his sleeping bag and groundsheet. His introduction to climbing had not yet deprived him of those comforts.

III
REPORTED MISSING

The dawn was clear, but sunrise was no surprise to me. At six I announced it was past ten and time to go. I stood up gratefully and stretched my aching limbs. I didn't realize the climbing above was so hard that five hours would pass before it was my turn to move off the ledge.

The route went straight up over the overhangs. Timo led again and needed five pitons and two *étriers* (five-foot ladders of nylon cord

69

with aluminum strips for steps) to make the first forty feet. From there on was another 120 feet of tough going to the ledge we should have reached the day before.

Bogel followed Timo, and we watched him leaning out backward over the drop to pull up over the first overhang. I glanced at Straub: "What do you think of that, Paul?"

"Hell, I don't know, Dave. I just hope it's not like that crack yesterday."

"No. This is something else. Forget the crack. This pitch will have holds here and there but very few. You must use them in the right sequence. Work it out before you make a move. But when you get to an overhang go over it fast or you'll tire very quickly."

The doctor climbed steadily, shouting for a tight rope now and then but avoiding the repeated falls of the crack. They would be waiting for him again on the next pitch.

As I went up to join him, we heard a small plane zooming in close. It was the Radio Caracas Cessna. Above us on the ledge Bogel took the radio from his climbing pack and talked to the pilot.

"We're a couple of hundred feet below you. Come down on your next pass and I'll fire off a red flare to mark our position."

Our slow pace on the first day had already led us to suspect that we would be on the face longer than we had estimated. The plane was the only link with our families and we were anxious to please the cameramen so they would keep returning.

Perched on a little stance, Straub and I waved

70

our arms wildly. Up above on the ledge Timo shook out his light blue parka and waved that. But at this point the weather closed in.

Several times in the following days we heard the plane in the clouds, but each time we were on difficult rock and nobody had his hands free to get the radio out. For a full eight days the plane got nothing from us but silence, and by then the Press was reporting us as missing.

IV

HOW TO TRAVEL FASTER

We now reached the first and largest of the two major ledges of the wall. More than 1,000 feet long, it cut horizontally across the face like a brilliant green scar, visible for miles. It was not a flat ledge but sloped steeply outward like the roof of a verandah running along the side of a house. Its thick vegetation, loose surface and steep angle made movement along it awkward and strenuous. The second great ledge started 500 feet above the north end of the first. It too could be seen from miles away running diagonally up the wall from left to right. The slope of its surface is very steep. In parts it was little more than a slight easing of angle from the verticality of the rock wall above and below it. But as with its neighbor below, the tenacious tropical greenery had occupied every inch of it.

The rock above looked unclimbable and we had to traverse a full 200 yards to the right be-

71

fore we found the first feasible line up it. This was a nasty twenty-foot-high wall that overhung at the top. Bogel, a specialist at this sort of obstacle, struggled hard but got stuck two-thirds of the way. Finally Timo swarmed up a thin, leafless sapling below and to the left of the wall and crossed from its topmost twigs to the rock and up to a stance. With a rope from him, Bogel and I forced the wall with difficulty and hauled the packs.

As Timo and Bogel continued on, I called to Straub to start up. He had climbed several overhangs that morning but we had used *étriers* on them and the rock had been clean. This wall was wet and slimy and there was nowhere to put a piton to hold an *étrier*. Straub was approaching his second trial.

My belay point was fifty feet above him and I could hear but not see his struggles below the overhang. I had taken in fifteen feet of rope when he shouted suddenly, "I'm coming off! Hold me! "

I braced hard and the rope burned briefly through my hands until I stopped him and he got back on the rock. He came up again slowly.

"I'm stuck under the overhang, Dave," he yelled. "I don't see how to do it."

A few seconds later his head appeared as he leaned out backward, clung on with one hand at waist level and reached up over the overhang with the other to scrabble desperately for a hold he couldn't see. It was as if he had climbed the arm of the Statue of Liberty and now had to pull up over the rim of the torch. Either he got

72

over it fast or he fell back exhausted. The doctor wasn't fast enough.

"Look out, Dave. I'm falling! "

He dropped out of sight and the rope cut into my hands and back. He got back onto the rock and we both paused a few minutes to regain our breath. Then he made his third attack, up fifteen feet to the overhang, only to fall once more. This time I could feel my legs buckling under the strain. As soon as he was back on the rock I shouted down that Timo had come up a tree on the left and crossed from it to the rock.

Straub hadn't seen this performance because he was still lugging packs along the ledge. I let out enough rope for him to descend and go around to the tree, and shortly he was gasping and shouting up to me, "How the hell . . . did he . . . reach the rock off this?"

Leaning over the edge, I saw a big, thickly leaved tree, a far cry from Timo's puny sapling, flailing around violently twenty feet from the rock. Exhausted as I was from holding him in so many falls, I couldn't help laughing.

"Paul! Monkey! You're up the wrong tree!"

There was a more costly incident in Straub's schooling to come. Timo came back down to take over the rope and I went on up to where a series of cracks and chimneys split a vertical section of 200 feet. I was moving carefully up this on my own, following the fixed rope left by Bogel, when I froze. There were shouts of alarm from below and the sound of someone or something falling. In the same instant I realized that daylight was fading.

"John! Paul!" I yelled. "Are you okay?"

I was starting down when I heard Timo's shout: "Paul's pack is lost. Gone over the edge."

That's great, I thought. Straub was now left with nothing but what he wore: pants and a T-shirt. No parka, no sleeping bag, no ground-sheet. He had even lost the box for his contact lenses. And this was only the second day.

But it didn't faze the doctor. From way below Timo his voice rose faintly: "Forget it. I can travel faster without baggage."

V

NIGHT CLIMBING

The water had fallen too, although Timo hadn't said so, and he had roped down three pitches in a desperate search for it before dark. He found it and dragged it—forty-five pounds of deadweight—back up the face. This gut-tearing work exhausted him, but he had pulled the expedition out of crisis.

I was standing on a hold just big enough for both feet and, in the last of the light, I leaned out to look up at the route. I could see nothing beyond an overhang fifteen feet above. That's going to be a real bastard in the dark, I thought.

I heard scraping on the rock below and rasping breath. It was Timo.

"Dave?"

"Up here, John. Just above you."

He struggled up a little farther and gasped, "Grab this. . . . It's the water. . . . Careful."

Holding the fixed rope I squatted on my book-size foothold and leaned down, feeling in the dark. I found the canvas bag holding the container, gripped it, straightened up and jammed it between my body and the rock. Then I worked myself sideways a few inches until I had only one foot on the hold.

"Come up on my right. You'll find room for one boot. But hurry. The water is pushing me off."

Presently Timo was beside me, both of us balancing on a perch scarcely big enough for one.

"Quick, John. I'll hold you while you tie the water on the rope."

I gripped the rope high with my left hand and held Timo into the rock with my right. He let go of the rope, reached down for the slack, tied a rapid overhand loop and clipped it into the kara-biner at the top of the canvas bag. Then he reached up and grabbed the rope again. With the weight of the water off me I whistled with relief.

"Now what?"

"We're in trouble, Dave. We need the third rope and Paul has it down below. We can't bring him up here. . . . There's no belay and there's no room for him."

There was no light either. Jammed up against Timo I could barely see the shape of his head. The moon would not reach us until later, and then only if the clouds cleared and we got out from the shadow of the great rock buttress on our right.

I could feel my right leg beginning to shake under my weight, and the first little flash of panic hit me. Panic and incredulity. Trapped *here*? I don't believe it. Stand on this miserable saucer of a foothold for *ten hours* until dawn? It would wreck us. Our alternative was to slide down the rope in the dark. But even if we found a ledge, we'd be separated from our sleeping kit and food. And what if it rained?

Suddenly I remembered.

"Hey, John. There's a small tree. Over to your right. I saw it just before dark."

"Where, Dave? Can I reach it?"

I fumbled behind Timo for the rope leading down to Straub, pulled up a few feet of slack, clipped it through the karabiner holding the water bag and put it in his hand. It would give some protection if he fell.

"John, I'll lean out left as you lean right for the tree."

With my right foot jammed against Timo's left we fell apart like two hinged poles and gradually increased the angle: two antic acrobats without any audience. I could hear Timo grunting as he flailed about feeling for the tree.

"I got it! It's great! Three inches thick at the root! "

With a firm grip on the tree he hauled me back upright and then let himself swing under it. I gave a careful sideways hop so that I had both feet on the ledge. After sharing it, it felt like a penthouse terrace.

Reaching the tree had changed the odds against us. Night climbing is normally impossible; you cannot see the route ahead and even

76

your immediate moves are difficult to judge. But now we had a belay as well as a fixed rope, and Bogel was already at the top of the pitch. With these aids we could risk it.

Timo found a ledge on the other side of the tree, rigged the belay, and Straub began his blind scrabble upward. "How about that, Dave?" said Timo. "His second day and he's climbing in the dark?"

We heard Bogel slithering down the fixed rope to the overhang above us: "What the hell's going on down there? Where are you guys?"

Straub reached the tree and we were ready for the next move. Bogel's voice came again: "Listen. It's moderate rock above this overhang and getting to it isn't so bad. Dave's the lightest. If he comes next and scrabbles a bit I'll heave him over the top and we'll both pull the next man up."

First he hauled the water and I followed, clawing and scratching up to the overhang and over it. Soon all four of us were up panting and cursing. Somewhere below we had left Timo's climbing pack. In it were pitons, karabiners and the expanding bolts. There was nothing we could do about it.

"I'll go first and run out the second rope behind me," Bogel said. "Then I'll haul the water with it and you can start up the fixed rope."

Above us we could see a glimmer of hazy moonlight on the rocks. The climbing was not difficult from here, though we jostled groggily against each other on the stances, four bone-weary blotches in the night who had been on the move sixteen hours and climbing in the dark for four. We stumbled at last into a wet two-foot-wide crack that ran back fifteen feet into the mountain before dropping off into a deep hole.

Bogel stood at the entrance. "Welcome to the Ritz, you guys," he said.

VI

EMPTY POCKETS

He had been at the bivouac since afternoon and had collected a heap of fuel to brighten our arrival. There couldn't have been a shrub left on the face. He had even traversed into some remote gully and brought back tree branches. In no time at all we had a fire going and could see the red, wet walls of our shelter rising into darkness.

I had an uncanny sense of being prehistoric, for we were the first men in that cave and the first to bring fire to it. In any case we looked like Stone Age men. In a few more days we would smell like them too.

While some Noble Soul was heating supper I went to the back of the crack and said, "Quiet. I'll drop a stone down to see how deep the hole is. . . . Now! "

I thrust my arm over the hole but kept the stone in my hand. Everyone counted wordlessly, one, two, three, four—there was horrified amazement on their faces in the firelight—five . . . At this point I dropped the stone, and two seconds later a faint crack and thud sounded from below.

"Good God, that must be *hundreds* of feet down," I said, beginning to believe it myself.

We needed a good meal that night and we got it. A large pan of beef and vegetable stew, some crumbly pancake and a big pot of hot limeade with tea bags thrown in. We left not a scrap. The pans, even the insides of the powder packets, were cleaned out.

We turned in on the damp rocky floor at one o'clock in the morning, Bogel to the rear, Timo to the front and Straub and I jammed head to foot in the middle. We had to lie on our sides, and once down we couldn't turn for the rest of the night. Through my garbage bag I could feel Straub shivering beside me.

"How's the climbing going, Paul?" I said.

"I guess I didn't do so well on that crack and the overhang," Straub answered. "I'm sorry I held you guys up. But I think it's great."

We were silent in the oozing darkness.

"Anyway, there's not much more this mountain can take from me," he laughed after a while. "Hell, even my pockets are empty."

FRONTAL
ATTACK FIEND

FIVE

Every expedition has its gung-ho ball of fire, the frontal-attack fiend with a perpetual itch for the hardest route in sight. Ours was George Bogel, for whom the proper route was the direct route, and the hazards be damned.

Bogel was a tireless worker with hard, high-altitude experience in the Andes, and within months of our own climb he was off to attack the 22,200-foot peak Huascarán in Peru. He was a radical, a type you get in any climbing generation, eager to dump tradition for the ultra-modern techniques, the sort to stir up a sedate climbers' club and infuriate the old boys. I'm no conservative myself, but if the expedition had lasted much longer Bogel and I would have tangled. It would have blown over quickly for basically we were one of a kind. But after long years of climbing I was inclined to look twice at risk whereas Bogel was still indifferent to it.

One of his prime talents was a total contempt for heights. He would sit unbelayed on the edge of a drop, legs dangling in space, and lean out with his head beyond his knees to haul a heavy pack. It wasn't nonchalance; he simply did not notice the exposure.

He was also impatient of slow pace or hesitation in others, and he had a temper. The wall of Angel Falls had never known a human voice before we got there. It knows one now. Bogel's roaring and cussing were enough to give birth to a new Indian legend.

I

ROUTE-FINDING

The third day of our ascent began with the first steep vegetation pitch of the wall, a stretch of 150 feet leading to a good ledge. Vegetation makes dangerous climbing. It can be vertical and often clings to no more than a thin layer of mud on the rock. Sometimes when you put your weight on it, it peels off in heavy, soggy sheets. The plants on this face were thick, fleshy grasses and a type of small aloe with lance-tipped, spiny-edged leaves. Nothing was secure and we had to move fast and keep our weight distributed evenly on all holds. You can afford a slip on rock if you have one reasonable handhold. On vegetation you cannot, for there is nothing to hold you. Moreover, with a four-man team, the first two climbers pull out what few stable holds are available, leaving none for the last two.

Timo was a master at this sort of climbing and he led off. Bogel followed and with help from the rope and our fingernails Straub and I made it too.

Once on the ledge we reviewed our tactics. "The rock directly above us is impossible," Timo said. "We have two alternatives. Either we go along the second and last main ledge of the wall which starts over on the right or we go left toward the falls and hope to find a more direct route."

"We go left," said Bogel shortly. "We've done enough damn traversing away from the falls. We're rock climbers aren't we? What the hell do you want? A goddamn staircase?"

"Wait a minute," Timo said. "Let's work it out. The rock there is very difficult. We might be days climbing a few hundred feet and then get stopped by some huge overhang. But we might run into trouble going right too because the lie of the rock there looks as though it might form a pinnacle detached from the main plateau. Once we're committed to either line it'll be our last chance. We haven't enough rations to make another try."

"We can't risk finishing on a pinnacle," Bogel said. "Better we prospect to the left for a clear line to the top. If we can't find one, we come back and go right."

We agreed to this and Timo and Bogel traversed left along a ledge. An hour later they returned defeated. We would have to go right.

As they got back to us, Timo was placating Bogel: "Take it easy, George. There *is* one final chance. There's a ledge leading left a few hundred feet up from here. I don't even know if we can reach it; we may have to swing across on a rope. But once we're there, we may find a route. If not, the odds are we end up on a pinnacle."

"We'll get across if we have to swing fifty

feet," said Bogel. "We're losing time talking about it. Let's *go,* damn it! Let's get *moving*!"

It was vintage Bogel, seven words we seized on with delight and adopted as the expedition's motto:

"Let's *go,* damn it! Let's get *moving*!"

II

JUMARS

Grabbing the packs, we traversed over to the second of the two great ledges of the wall. Steep and loose, it was hard work. We had to lift the packs above our heads, hold them against the slope, kick a foothold in the soaking vegetation or loose scree and step up. Then heave the packs up again. One step, one heave. Sixty pounds per man, for a hundred yards.

At the end of it we faced a thirty-foot rampart overhung with two feet of solid vegetation as tough and springy as bamboo. It was like a prison wall topped with barbed wire. Timo had to use four pitons and two *étriers* to climb it. Bogel followed, removed the pitons, dropped a fixed rope and leaned over:

"You're on your own, you guys. Use the jumars. They're in the small pack."

He vanished upward to join Timo on the next pitch.

Down at the bottom Straub and I stared at each other. Jumars? Even Timo had never used them. We had never even *seen* one. We dug them out and examined them warily. Jumars were originally designed for extreme situations, such as rescue from a crevasse in a glacier or returning up a rope you have gone down only to find you have no place to land. They clip onto the rope and can be pushed upward but not downward. Downward pressure locks them onto the rope by a hinged, toothed gripping device.

The way to use them is to clip one karabiner into each of two jumars, then four-foot long loops of rope to the karabiners. You stand in one loop, shove the other jumar up the rope, transfer your weight to its loop and shove the lower one up. You should have a top rope to stop your fall in case the jumars slip off or the rope breaks, and should also attach yourself to the fixed rope with a third loop tied in a prusik knot above the jumars. A prusik knot works on the same principle as the jumars and allows the climber to hang from the loop and rest. We had no top rope and Straub had no prusik loop.

So we were to learn a new technique the hard way, in action and without a teacher. Straub went first moving straight up without a check until he got to that barbed-wire hedge at the top. The rope was buried in it, which prevented the jumars from sliding any farther. Straub gave it all he had but finally shouted for help from above. The Bogel Boom came rolling down the wall:

"Get your thumb out! Get your ass up over that thing!"

His voice was raging and Straub, startled, literally threw himself over the top. Immediately came the Bogel Blandishment: "You see, Paul.

Nothing like a yell to set the old adrenaline going."

It was an apology and the doctor accepted it with a good-humored shrug. I was relieved, for senior surgeons are not used to being cussed at like that and we could afford no personal confrontations.

I clipped the packs on the rope as Straub hauled, but somehow we forgot Timo's parka, a mistake which would cost him days of wet misery to come. Then I tied the last pack on the rope to steady it and started up. By good fortune I got the sequence right and was up quickly, marveling at the ingenuity of the jumars but well aware it would take nerve to trust their gripping mechanism over a long drop. We were to meet that test higher up the wall and our forced lesson was to prove vital.

A hundred and thirty feet above we found Timo standing on a flat boulder jammed into a tall cleft.

"Well, gentlemen," he said, "you can take your choice of bivouacs. There's a hole below me and there's one here. There's not much between them."

He was right. The lower offering was a den fit for a cold-blooded amphibian. The one above was just as dank and required climbing to get to. We slung the miry packs into the den. But we still had two hours of daylight and characteristically Bogel got fidgety. Finally he grabbed a rope and tied on:

"We'll never get up this goddamn face if we keep taking the first goddamn bivouac we see in the middle of the day. We out on a goddamn picnic or something?"

86

He started up the right side of the den in steadily worsening rain and forty feet up asked irritably why no one was following. Timo joined him while Straub and I ranged around for kindling. It was dusk before they returned, soaking wet, sliding down a rope they had fixed higher up.

Impatient Bogel, as it turned out, had made a good move. The next morning at dawn, Straub, unhappy about his slow pace of yesterday, ascended the fixed rope and heaved the packs up on his own. Timo followed him, and we had the hauling done and two men climbing before the mountain was awake.

III

HELLHOLE

The fourth day we climbed an endless series of slabs and muddy ledges in continuous rain. Then in the afternoon we bumped into a little wall that blocked us. It was only twelve feet high but covered with green slime except for its left end, which was streaming with water. After a moment Bogel's face lit up.

"The cliff-hangers! The pride of Californian hardware men," he said.

He rummaged in his bag and produced two outrageous pieces of gear. They were slivers of steel four inches long, a quarter-inch wide and bent over at the top. Reaching up, he hooked one onto a wrinkle in the rock. Then he attached a nylon web sling with loops in it for footholds.

Using this precarious aid, he moved up to a natural handhold and swarmed to the top.

"Try that, fellows," he chortled. "Scares the hell out of you. It's the unsafest gadget I know."

We made it up on his rope and manhandled the packs another sixty feet to a bivouac. This was to be the scene of a classic display of Bogel's nervelessness and our reaction to it spoke worlds about our mental state. The place was a four-foot-wide fissure in the rock with a roof thirty feet above and a dirt slope outside.

Inside to the right was a wide hole hidden in shadow. Straub discovered it, dropped a stone and turned to us, appalled:

"For God's sake, fellows, keep away from this. It must be 200 feet deep."

Bogel, rampaging around looking for sleeping space, wasn't listening. A second later he simply stepped backward into the hole and dropped out of sight. We leaped to our feet but froze when muffled curses rose from below. Bogel's shaved head appeared in the gloom. Then his hands, fumbling for holds on the rim. He crawled out so unconcernedly that Straub was indignant:

"Don't you know that hole goes down to Australia? It's twenty stories deep, man."

"Well, what *you* don't know is, there's a ledge about eight feet down."

Bogel stood there brushing himself off and we eyed him speculatively. We all had the same thing in mind.

"Hey, George," I said. "Next time you fall down a hellhole, and *if* we recover your corpse, how do we lower you down the face without scraping off what's left of your skin?"

"Oh, nuts, Dave."

"No. Listen now. What *do* we do if one of us falls? If he's killed, do we risk the others to get him down? Worse, suppose he's got multi-fractures but is still alive?"

We were silent a moment, even a little embarrassed, until a slow grin spread across Bogel's face.

"Well, if it's you, Dave, we'll leave you under a rock somewhere. . . . And now, how's about some grub?"

In truth, we had no answer to the problem, and it was the last time we were to mention it until the hazardous days of the descent.

IV

A VERY NASTY OBJECT

The night rain began with thudding drops and soon water was streaming down the rock outside. By God, I thought, the rain-catcher!

Putting on my parka, I scrambled down the slope with a plastic sheet. The downpour was so heavy I filled a pan by just holding it out, then passed it up to the others. I dug a hole in the mud and built a wall around it with rocks, pushed the middle of the sheet into it and secured the edges with stones. It was full in minutes. Above they had found a green shrub that fizzed and crackled on the fire, filling that spooky crack with light and cheeriness. But I was happy crouched in the rain, washing the

89

pots and drinking, filling the bottles and drinking again. The water problem was solved. The next morning we would have a fresh six gallons.

But back in the bivouac there was a less savory bit of business I had to face up to. I had an infected thumb. Two days before, dirt had been forced a quarter-inch under the nail in a desperate grab at a vegetation hold. The thumb had festered painfully and I couldn't use it. It was Doctor Straub's turn to cook, so I flicked open my switchblade knife, counted three and rammed it under the nail. I jumped and squawked as the pus welled out, and Bogel squirmed in disgust. The clowns were on stage once more.

"For God's sake, Dave. We're just going to eat."

But the relief was instant. I would now be able to tie a knot in the rope without yickering with pain. I probed until the blood ran cleanly.

"Get back out in the rain, will you!" Bogel yelled. "Go take a walk!"

I advanced on him with the knife: "Bogel. Your head needs shaving again."

But Straub's noodle soup was ready and peace was upon us.

You may be wondering what a respectable citizen like me was doing with a switchblade. The summer before I had bought it in France, where they are not prohibited, to slice up rations on my Alpine climbs. The implement was as short as a penknife but could be opened easily with cold, stiff fingers.

I told my companions how it had been taken from me at London Airport before boarding a flight to New York. I must have a hijacker's face. A police captain, one of those gentlemanly fellows you still find on the London police force, fished it out of my wife's handbag.

"What's this? How does it work?"

"Well . . . you just sort of press that little button there and . . ."

The police captain did and the blade flashed out wickedly. He examined the knife and me with disdain and handed it to a crew member for return to me at Kennedy Airport.

"That is a very nasty object," he said.

V

KIT LOSSES

After supper we stood over the fire steaming the wet mud out of our clothes and discussed how to fit into the small sleeping space. With memories of being jammed immovably between Straub and the rock the night before I elected to sleep outside, rain or no rain.

Before turning in we ran over our situation. Though we had been climbing four days, we were only at the 1000-foot level. According to Timo's plans we should have been at or near the top. Starting out on our fifth day we would still have two-thirds of the wall above us.

And now we discovered another problem. By some unforgivable oversight we had only one set of matches between us, a plastic container of thirty-year-old Lucifers belonging to Timo. He had brought them along more or less as a curiosity, but we now realized they were our sole source of fire. Later on we would starve for this mistake.

Then we began to list our kit losses. By the fourth day we had lost a lantern, a pack with all Straub's gear, Timo's climbing pack and parka, and one of the water tanks. Kit losses are inevitable on a long climbing expedition where anything you let go of drops out of sight. Most of our errors were due to being caught by darkness on a very complex and awkward route. Even so, we were hardly performing like veterans. Only wham-bang Bogel was not guilty. He snorted at us derisively:

"You're the worst set of bums I ever saw on a climbing rope. Losing kit all over the mountain."

We reminded him we were cool cats who still had nine lives and he'd lost one of his down the hellhole. But each of us, as the climb continued, had to swallow this counterclaim. We would all lose a couple of lives ourselves.

GRANDPA

SIX Trying to pack the duffelbag tightly next morning, I jerked it upright and was thumping it up and down when a jolt of pain shot through my arms. My fingers opened and the bag dropped. The signs were unmistakable. It was the Palsy. I remembered the Alps, the same spasm of pain, the glacier far below as I fell off the rock and swung on the rope.

I continued stuffing the kit into the bag like a robot, thinking fast. You're forty-two, Grandpa. If you want to live to be forty-three, you can't let this happen again.

The first trick was to stop hauling packs. But how could I, in all conscience, impose extra labor on the others? The second trick was to muster every bit of experience and skill I could. To climb cleanly, no blood-and-guts grab-and-pull. In other words, *concentrate,* no matter how dead beat I was.

I looked down at the duffel and saw it was as ragged as the rest of the packs. The contents were showing through the holes. I tied a barrel hitch around it and secured the rope, shoulder straps and flap ring to the karabiner.

"Up pack!" I yelled and watched the duffel jerking up the rock. My God, I thought, if I have to heave that thing one yard I'll be screwed for the day. I stood scratching my beard, trying to work it out.

"Say, Dave," Timo called down. "That's a great piece of packaging. Really secure." There was no irony in his voice.

"That's okay, John," I said absentmindedly. "Anytime."

"How about all the time? Would you mind? You tie and we'll haul?"

Well I'll be damned, I thought. Trick one.

I did a gleeful little jig on the bivouac floor, tied onto the rope and started up. Now, Grandpa, let's see about trick number two.

I

DISCOMFORTS

The route went through a slanting tunnel in the roof and the moss and slime were as thick as seaweed. We were drenched immediately. There is a world of difference between being wet with rainwater and being wet with mud and slime. With water, even if you are totally soaked, your clothes cling, they still have friction, you can run your hands down the front of your thighs and feel the rough texture of the cloth. But not with mud and slime. Running my hands over my legs I felt as if I had fallen into a tank of cold oil. In order to tie the duffelbag, I had to put my arms around it to turn it over because the material was too slimy to grip otherwise. Worse, the rope was in the same condition.

On the 1968 expedition to the Auyán-Tepuí, botanists found a sort of jelly on the ground among bromeliads and pitcher plants. This jelly is formed by a green alga. Later that day we were to gaze in disgust at blobs of it on the walls of a cleft we had to get up. For a climber, this stuff was deadly. We had to live with it on the wall, and sleep in it as well.

We suffered the normal climbing discomforts, too, of course. I have often been asked what you do about going to the john when jammed four to a little ledge. For a male climber, peeing over a drop even when standing on small holds is no problem at all. Many's the man who has sprinkled a pitch below that has cost him all his guts and strength to get up. Aha, you bastard, he says, that will teach you to fart in church. For the rest he must grab his chances. In this particular bivouac I seized the moment when Timo was heaving up the duffelbag. There was a hellhole at the back, after all.

You find on expeditions that temperament and training in this matter still count when most other habits give way to hard conditions. On our own climb, one of us gave no indication in ten days that he felt the call of nature at all. Another was occasionally seen to be discretely edging away out of sight. One showed a Gallic acceptance of the facts of life and, when the situation imposed it, of a total lack of camouflage. The fourth man behaved like a soldier in his fifth year of war. Whenever it hit him, he squatted. The well-I'll-be-damned looks of the rest of us didn't touch him. I shall leave the reader to guess who is who. For the logistically minded, we carried one toilet roll down the river. I didn't see it after that. Thereafter I relied on a penny notebook I carried in the flap of my pack to write the log in. How the others managed I haven't the faintest idea.

II

SOME PRACTICAL MEASURES

Above the roof of the bivouac there was 120 feet of varied climbing to the foot of a villainous sixty-foot chimney. A chimney is a fissure wider than a crack, wide enough to get most or all of your body inside. You jam your way up wedging yourself between the two walls. Some chimneys are too wide for this technique and you have to bridge them by spread-eagling your arms and legs across to holds on both sides. This one was twice as high as Straub's Crack, which we had encountered on our first day. It was also dripping with slime.

Timo, however, led up it like a master, without a slip. From then on we called it Timo's Chimney. Bogel went up next, and for some time we heard no sound from above. It was clear they had run into an even worse obstacle.

It was raining hard and Straub and I, immobilized at the bottom, were shaking with the cold. It was like one of those agonizing delays on ice-caked rock in a Scottish winter that knock the stuffing out of you if they draw on too long. I tried the old trick of controlled shivering, where you encourage your body to tremble violently and then relax suddenly to gain a second or two of warmth. The warmth is probably illusory, but it helps.

We regaled each other with tales of icy times gone by, and I recalled a freight-train-hopping escapade as a schoolboy in Britain during World War II. I jumped an ammunition train one wintry Saturday night and found myself in an open wagon filled with artillery shells. I fell asleep during that miserable ride and woke to find my hands frozen to the shells. On Monday morning, I had to tell some devious story to my teachers, otherwise . . . Your hands got stuck to a *what*? You were riding on a *what*? Give him six strokes across the backside!

"There were no school psychiatrists in those days," I told Straub.

"C'mon now, Dave. Save that old-days stuff for the other two. I'm thirty-eight remember."

"Wait another four years and you'll see what I mean. But seriously now, I'm slowing down badly. I'm not fit enough for this wall."

"Nonsense. You're getting up the damn thing, aren't you?"

"Just barely, Paul. I got the Palsy today. I don't want to worry John about it."

Straub pointed to my arms, "Tendons, again? Well," he offered, "I'll see that I stay third on the rope and if you get in trouble I'll heave you up."

"Thank you, Doc. That's what I call practical medicine."

From above we were told they were ready. Up Straub went and I shivered on, arms out like a penguin, trying not to come in contact with my cold, slimy clothes. Then down came word to tie on the packs, so I jumped at the big duffelbag and wrestled around with it in the mud, tying it up viciously with the oozing rope. Up it went and the rope came whistling down for the rest.

"Up pack!"

Now it was my turn, and just a few feet of that jelly-smeared chimney had me steaming with effort. An alarming pitch, this one, and about fifty feet up I looked straight down to the jungle some 1,200 feet below.

I pulled out at the top, coiled the rope and went on with Straub to join the others up seventy-five feet of easy scrambling. I was about to congratulate Timo on his lead when I was stopped by the sight of Bogel in a real fight-to-the-death thirty feet up the next pitch.

It was a smooth face with a big overhang at the top. The only way up was at the left edge, but here the overhang was impossible to climb. Ten feet to the right it jutted out less and gave a better chance. But there was no direct route to this point. The only possibility was to ascend on the left and traverse those ten feet under the overhang. The sole hope of pulling off this feat was an inverted crack between the overhang and the face. It was a mean obstacle.

Bogel was hanging with his left hand thrust above his head into the crack and feeling with his right for another hold. Timo called up tensely: "Give it all you've got, George. Fight it. We can't be stopped now." But there wasn't another hold.

Bogel hammered a piton upward into the

crack, attached a foot loop and stood in it. He hammered in a piton farther along, clipped in a foot loop and stepped across into it. It was a horribly insecure process. Struggling along to where the overhang jutted out two feet, he reached over it desperately for holds. This was the crux of the pitch and Bogel was in a dangerous position. But his violent style came through and in one magnificent thrust he got over. It was a genuine souped-up performance and we yelled and whooped to cheer him on. If ever another expedition follows the Timo Route they may find the pitch dry, but it will still be a serious problem. Wet and slimy, it was vicious.

It was getting dark when my turn came. Timo called down proposing that all hands man the rope and pull me up to save time. This was reasonable, but there was a note of mischief I'd missed. No sooner did I say I was ready than I shot straight up four feet, then another four feet. I was moving so fast I couldn't push off from the rock and scraped up like the duffelbag, hitting the overhang with a thud. I weigh maybe 147 when mud-caked, and this is peanuts to three hardened pack haulers anxious to find a hole in the rock before night.

III

SLEEPING PILLS

A hundred feet farther up we found a twenty-five-foot tooth of rock leaning forward over the slope with a jumble of sharp-edged boulders at its foot. Despite my rapid ascent it was now dark. Our overhanging rock was dry as a bone on its underside, pure pink, unmossed, unslimed sandstone. And it was *dry*. Timo and I found shrubs and lit a fire while Bogel and Straub wrestled with the jagged boulders to make some sort of sleeping area. I found mine in a narrow, four-foot-long trough between the rocks. For once we were free of ooze and mud.

Straub, shivering in his T-shirt, perched himself on a flake of rock close under the roof and directly above the fire. Eyes closed and scarcely breathing in the smoke, he stuck it out until he was steaming. The Noble Souls for the night were Timo and Bogel who, in the firelight, dug out our grimy food packets, peered at the instructions and produced a series of hot somethings that had us all mooing with relief and gratitude.

By now personal mess-tins were out of fashion. When something was ready in the two-quart pot it went around the circle while each of us took four or six sips according to the instructions of the cook and disher-outer. Three pairs of eyes watched every move of whomever had the pot and occasionally there would be a joking grumble of reproof: "That wasn't a sip. That was a long drag."

The pan would go around perhaps three times, and each time the remaining amount was measured by the cook and the new number of sips announced. There was never a squabble. No one ever went over his ration. Those who were not being Noble Souls, the Abject Beings, would sit in torpidness, as close to the fire as possible, nursing bruises and cuts and aching joints. When told, they would reach out with their swollen, muddy fingers, take the warm pot and, groaning with pleasure, take the allotted number of sips and pass it on with no attempt at a sneaky extra.

The night was distinctly colder. This was welcome confirmation that we were gaining altitude, but it did not alleviate a chill in the back while facing the fire, and vice-versa. For me, a chronic insomniac with only a plastic bag for protection, increasing cold was bad news that could only get worse as we approached the rim of the mountain, 5,900 feet above sea level.

Counting the night at the foot of the wall, this was our seventh rough bivouac and I was beginning to feel the lack of sleep. I had noticed that when I glanced down from a foot- or handhold to the jungle,—now thousands of feet below,—my eyes would not immediately change focus. This split second of hazy vision was unnerving and dangerous.

To combat the problem I now decided to take two of Timo's sleeping pills. With Timo draped across the boulders in his unslung hammock and the others twisted around the lumps in their spot below, I drifted off into an unpleasant limbo filled with thumpings and sudden flashes of light and surfaced from it three hours later with bone-rattling shivers. Thoroughly doped, I felt around for twigs for the fire, blew it into flames and subsided against the warm stone it was perched on. The rest of the night was divided between fragmented nightmares and ineffective puffing at a dying fire.

IV

THE VEGETABLE

Day six was crucial, for we were close to the high point of the 1969 attempt. We had had five full days of climbing, time and strength were running out and tactics had to be scrupulously considered.

We could try to force the pitch which had stopped the last expedition, in which case we risked ending up on a pinnacle cut off from the main face, or we might traverse left along a ledge, drop a fixed rope sixty feet in an attempt to reach a second ledge and traverse this to search out another route closer to the falls. This was a major problem of route-finding. Detailed photographs of this part of the face are few, so there was little to guide us, and we could not tell whether the second ledge was directly below the first.

And there were other questions. If we reached the second ledge and found a route farther to the left, what would we do with the fixed rope? If we left it, would we need it higher up? If we pulled it down and took it with us, would we be able to climb back up or would we have cut off our retreat? One mistake could cause a crisis.

But there was an immediate crisis. Me. I was freaked out. Timo's sleeping pills had been dynamite. I was floating four feet above and to the left of myself. The bivouac, the sky and the mountain were a blurry haze.

"Hold it, you blokes," I slurred. "I'm not

quite with it . . . dizzy. . . . Bloody pills, I guess. . . . Can't see straight."

They stared with concern as I shook myself, trying to clear my head.

"I knew you shouldn't have taken two, Dave," said Timo. "Do you think you can move at all? We can't leave you here, because we might not be coming back this way."

"No . . . you go on . . . I'll follow."

After a moment's hesitation, Timo and Bogel moved off and I tottered groggily after them. Straub was close behind me with a firm grip on my rope.

Heading left from the bivouac, we traversed across a gully, around the corner at its far side, along fifty feet of vegetated ledge, where we crossed under the critical 1969 highpoint, rigged our fixed rope and slid down to land safely on the second ledge. This was a tense moment. Timo had pondered for two years whether this maneuver was possible, whether the slide down the rope would bring us to the lower ledge or to nothing.

Meanwhile, for me, the junkie of the party, each stop brought me to a nothing of my own. I would keel over and drowse off. Typical of our luck from the beginning, the weather was clear for only the second time in eight days, just when I needed cold, sluicing rain to bring me around. I was too doped even to untie the rope and take off my parka in the heat. The dry-mouth effect of the pills increased to an intense thirst, but there would not be a sip of water until we bivouacked eight or ten hours later. I was in a wretched state: the expedition Vegetable.

At one point I opened my eyes to find myself perched on the side of a gully whose opposite wall was gray and sinister. It was only forty feet across from me and swept up for hundreds of feet. When I leaned out I could see that this wall ended in space hundreds of feet below, cutting back into the face in a colossal overhang. Far below that was the jungle. I realized the wall I clung to was its horrible twin and I should have felt the exciting kick that exposure gives an alert and healthy climber. Instead I ducked my head and vomited.

V

ONE NIGHT'S SLEEP

After a while I looked up blearily and saw Timo and Bogel coming down the gully. It had proved unclimbable.

"How do you feel, Dave?"

"Drunk."

"Must have been that iced melon you had for breakfast," said Bogel.

"How about it, Paul?" said Timo.

"He's got the shakes. I'll stay with him while you two prospect further on."

Timo and Bogel traversed the bottomless giant opposite us on into the next, equally intimidating gully. They came back three hours later with Bogel looking thoughtful, almost subdued.

"Damn it. I should have gone straight at it."

"You don't have to blame yourself for retreating," said Timo.

"But there were little ledges way up. Damnit, if only I hadn't hesitated."

Grabbing me by my waist loop, Straub pushed me gently back along the ledge.

"Well, let's go find a bivouac. This patient needs a head transplant."

Once out of the gully and back on the main face we found a horizontal fissure in the rock two feet high that would keep us out of the rain. By now I was feverish and dizzy and sat with my head between my knees. The doctor gave me some pills from his medicine bag and told me to turn in. Now this really was luxury. I was allotted the flat edge of the fissure, which otherwise sloped upward toward the back. Straub took over my garbage bag and I found myself under the damp but warm, unzipped sleeping bag that Straub and Bogel had started sharing the night before. I was fed royally where I lay, and later Bogel, who took the other berth under the sleeping bag, spent a miserable night struggling to avoid rolling down on top of the patient. So Straub had his problems with the plastic bag and its clammy condensation, Bogel with gravity, Timo with his worry about tomorrow's route and all three with the knowledge that the next day was the crux in the assault and that one of the group was sick.

Meantime the sick man was supremely oblivious to it all, snoring. This was all I needed: one night's sleep. Not much to ask for once a week. The sole penalty, as Bogel put it, was that the alarm clock didn't go off at dawn as usual. I failed to wake until 7:30 that morning, but did so with an extra clatter to drive away the others' fear that they had a nonstarter on their hands. The Vegetable was fit again.

SOMETHING OF
A MOUNTAINEER

"I need not say," said our leader, "that on the occasion of my last visit I exhausted every means of climbing the cliff, and where I failed I do not think that anyone else is likely to succeed, for I am something of a mountaineer. I had none of the appliances of a rock climber with me, but I have taken the precaution to bring them now."

So boasts George Edward Challenger, egomaniacal hero of *The Lost World*. Conan Doyle's novel is an entertaining melodrama of dinosaurs and pterodactyls but his hero's statement, if not the man's passionate immodesty, might speak for our own expedition leader's determination to reach the top of the "Lost World."

John Timo had made two attempts to climb the face of Angel Falls and had failed both times. Four years of work and dreams lay behind this third attempt. It was clear on our seventh day of climbing, as we approached and passed the highpoint of the 1969 expedition, that he would not be stopped easily, not even if it meant, as we were to discover, a dive into space.

But first, to start the morning off, Bogel insisted on one more attack against the gully wall that had repulsed him the previous afternoon.

I

BOGEL'S ATTEMPT

This was a serious undertaking, the sort of route a crack climbing team might attempt in good weather on an accessible cliff they could retreat from if they failed, then go home and return the following weekend. They would name it Undertaker's Wall or Hangman's Slab, and if they got stuck on it the local club would be out in a flash to rescue them, swarming down from the top with 1,000 feet of rope and the happy knowledge that press photographers were zeroing in with telephoto lenses. But for us there could be no rescue, and with our short rations, no return. If we failed it would be the end of the expedition.

"But if we make it, there's no danger of ending up on a pinnacle," Bogel said as we packed up, our packs scraping on the bright red and yellow sandstone bivouac floor. "That's the one argument you can't get around."

He stared at each of us in turn, rattling his pitons, psyched up and ready to go.

"I could've made a good start on it yesterday but I hesitated. . . . You know how it is . . . lost my drive. But I'll go straight at it today . . . you'll see. Come on, let's try it."

We were wavering, getting wound up ourselves, glancing at each other with little excited grins. Bogel saw the signs and took advantage:

"Well let's *go,* damn it! Let's get *moving*!"

We traversed the first gully, around its far wall into the second. It was cloudy but not raining.

Soon we were strung out along a narrow ledge, the rock against our right shoulders, the drop beneath our left boots. The belay was rigged and Bogel checked his equipment—slings and *étriers,* hammer and pitons. Then with Timo paying out the rope, he inched up eight, ten feet on tiny holds. I ran my eyes up the wall hundreds of feet into the clouds, then down over the edge below.

If George makes even fifty feet we'll be committed once and for all, I thought. There will be nowhere to stand for maybe two days. We'll be hanging from pitons night and day. Well, Nott, you bloody well got yourself into this, so . . . Suddenly a slithering sound from above. I jerked up to see Bogel falling, spread-eagled in space.

He hit the ledge, bounced off it . . . and somehow stopped himself with his two palms smacking on the ledge. It was like an astonishing circus trick. We gaped at him clinging there like a puppet on a picture rail.

Instantly he pulled himself up and attacked again. Not a word, not a change of expression. He might have stumbled off his front-door step. We watched him as he forced his way up ten or twelve feet . . . and fell once more, thudded onto the ledge and shot over the drop. Timo braced himself, gripped the rope and took the shock faultlessly. Bogel had fallen twenty-five feet and we could hear him scuffling about below.

In a few minutes he was heaving himself onto the ledge, not a scratch on him.

"That's it, George," said Timo firmly. "Let's try the cracks. What do you say, gentlemen?"

"For God's sake, yes," I said. "We can't get strung up on a wall when George falls off its first twelve feet *twice.*"

109

"Paul?"

"Well, I'm no expert but it looks damn dicy to me."

We turned to Bogel, who was leaning against the rock panting. His face was set and he said nothing. Timo put a hand on his shoulder. "Let's go, George."

II

"BONG, BABY . . ."

We traversed back across the wall, along under the bivouac site and over to the rope we had fixed the day before. We were subdued, and our morale wasn't helped by the unearthly vegetation at the back of the gully. It was fleshy and lurid, so green the air was green. Totally alien, it increased our feeling that we had entered a prehistoric world.

I glanced back and gave a sudden, Oscar-winning shriek: "George! What's that thing behind you?"

Bogel jerked around nervously in the green gloom, but all he saw was Straub's grin. "Damn it," he growled at me, his old self again.

We swarmed up the sixty feet of fixed rope to the higher ledge. From there Timo and Bogel went ahead with the climbing gear, leaving Straub and me to handle the packs. Ferrying these up, we had time to study the route ahead. It was obviously tough and we had already wasted half the day.

What confronted us was a sheer, deep-red wall that swept up 130 feet to a large overhang and continued on in jutting noses that vanished in the clouds. The rock was hard and smooth, changing in color above the overhang from red to pale pink to gray. It was unclimbable. On the right was a 100-foot chimney, also impossible, plastered with slime. Farther to the right were the steep cracks and walls that had turned back the last expedition. It was the only line we could take.

"See that crack fifty feet up?" Timo pointed. "That's what stopped me two years ago. It's too wide to hold a piton." Opening a pack he removed what Conan Doyle's hero would no doubt have referred to as one of those "appliances of a rock climber."

"I hope we can do it with this," he said.

He was holding a bong—a V-shaped, springy sheet of steel like a paperback-novel page folded lengthwise, its edges two inches apart, with several holes to clip karabiners into. When you reach a holdless section in a crack too wide for a piton, you hammer in a bong, clip in a karabiner with an *étrier* hanging from it and climb the steps of the ladder until you reach holds farther up. It is a maneuver both strenuous and delicate.

Bogel flicked the bong with his thumb. "Bong, baby," he admonished, "you better behave."

All our hopes centered on this single piece of metal with the comical name, a name that comes from the musical sound it makes as you hammer it in, a sound that rises in pitch if the bong is going in true and solid. The question was, would this one hold in the crack above?

Timo checked his equipment and, with the tiniest nod to us, started up. He climbed carefully. A short wall, a crack, a step to the left, gaining height steadily. At fifty feet he paused. Then in one, two quick moves he was at grips with the crack. Awkwardly perched, he felt at his back for the sling carrying his pitons—and the bong.

He removed the latter, reached up and hammered it in. Slowly his hand returned to his equipment, withdrew a karabiner and an *étrier* and clipped them in. We watched as he eased his foot onto the ladder, glanced down once and placed his weight on it.

Here we go, I thought. If the bong slips out, John splits his head and breaks a leg or two.

But he climbed the *étrier* swiftly until he could grip the karabiner at waist level. Finding a hold above it, he lifted his foot onto the bong and stepped up boldly, fighting his way up the crack and out of it onto a minuscule stance. Below, we cheered. The bong had worked. Timo was above the 1969 highpoint.

III

DIVE INTO SPACE

But above the crack the rock did not ease off, it grew worse. Thirty feet higher, Timo was forced onto a left traverse so precarious it may rate technically as the hardest section of the entire 3,282-foot route. It led him to a large block jammed at the top of the 100-foot chimney.

This block, five feet wide, had dangerously sharp edges and it was to be the support belay for more loads and lives than I care to remember. Beyond it, on the edge of the Red Wall, was a small triangle of earth. Timo belayed here and Bogel climbed up to him. A lengthy silence followed. It was a sign of trouble, as always, and the prelude to a bold, hair-raising move by Timo.

First a rope was dropped to hang directly down the chimney, without touching its sides. Then Bogel's voice called faintly: "Rope secured—Paul—jumar up." Each word was punctuated with a gap and we listened intently as the message was repeated. We were to jumar up 100 feet of rope swinging free in space, without a protecting rope from above. The rope was slimy and there was no guarantee the jumars would not slip off. I recalled the great climbers who had died when their fixed ropes broke, the American John Harlin on the Eiger, the Englishman Tom Patey, the Austrian Hermann Bühl and many others. Bogel and Timo knew these risks, so there must be a serious reason for the tactic they had chosen.

"Well, Paul," I said. "We had one lesson with jumars down below. Now we're in the big league."

Straub started up. Caked in mud, he looked like the victim of a trench collapse. Whenever he rested in his slings, head slumped forward to keep his balance, he twirled slowly, his limbs motionless, and I had the macabre notion that he was a corpse being *lowered* down that sinister cleft.

Disturbed by this image, I moved to the edge

of the Red Wall and looked up to see Timo precariously perched above the overhang 130 feet up. I noticed he had two ropes tied to his waist. So that's why they couldn't spare one to protect us, I thought. But what the hell are they up to?

I also saw that the only line of advance from his level was a steep vegetated corner to the left. But to get to it he had to traverse forty feet across a sheer wall. The wall overhung the whole face and beneath him was a clear drop of 2,600 feet to the jungle. This was far from a normal situation. Few climbs in the world are so exposed. It was in this appalling spot that Timo was to make his dive into space.

He started the traverse on a narrow ledge. After eight feet it petered out and he crept across a line of finger- and toeholds. I could see by his pace that these holds got progressively smaller until they vanished. The last ten feet of the traverse was smooth—totally unclimbable. He had been far too long on such tiny holds and I found myself tensed, whispering, "Get back, man! Get back before you fall!"

Still he hung, and I could see his limbs begin to shake with strain. "Go back, John!" I exploded. "Get . . ." I stopped abruptly. One moment Timo was clinging there, the next he was leaping, arms outstretched, across that ten-foot gap to the corner.

What he landed on was a near perpendicular slope of mud and grass that looked as safe to hang from as your living-room draperies. He dug his fingers in, feet scrambling for purchase, and incredibly the sod held. Then, after a pause, he climbed swiftly thirty feet to a belay.

Timo's own explanation, later, for his feat was the essence of simplicity: "There was no other way."

IV

INTO THE ABYSS

I was still staring upward in disbelief when Straub shouted that he was up the chimney and it was my turn to go. I tied my pack onto the bottom of the fixed rope as anchor and clipped on the jumars that had come whizzing and clinking down. Fifty feet up was the bong, five yards to my right. It was the only one we had and it was my job to rescue it. I began to swing back and forth, pushing off from the left wall of the chimney. With each swing I came closer and got so worked up about reaching it I forgot that what I was doing could jerk the jumars off the rope at any second. I also failed to notice that dusk was approaching.

Meantime, Timo had tied one end of the 200-foot rope to his belay while Bogel anchored the other to the big block above the chimney. The rope hung across the wall as a fixed line from which packs—and we—could be dangled from slings and hauled across with Timo's second rope to the other side. This unnerving setup is called a Tyrolean.

The first to try the airy ride was Straub and his voice was the first to reach me in half-an-hour. But his message was for the Almighty, not for me. It said, echoing forlornly down the wall: "I'm fa-a-a-lling!"

The shout jerked me back to reality. The hell with the bong. It was near dark and we had been trapped again, with me halfway up the chimney, Bogel on the little ledge, Straub falling off the traverse and Timo way up somewhere in the muddy corner.

By the time I got up the chimney, Straub had thumped into the corner with a pull from Timo and both were hauling the packs across. The doctor had yelled in alarm because he was unused to the elasticity of nylon rope. When his weight had come on the line it had stretched frighteningly.

I joined Bogel on the ledge and my boots sank deep into mire. It was a thoroughly insecure, nasty lump of earth wobbling over the drop. I still knew nothing of the fixed line and goggled in the darkness when Bogel told me.

There is always a moment on a big climb when it hits you personally that there is no retreat. Like a paratrooper who has stepped up to the door of the plane, you cannot draw back even if you are sick with fright. I knew these clutches of panic were momentary because I often have them. You just have to get a grip on yourself. But now that grip was eluding me.

The rain had started and we were shivering. Bogel guided my hand to the fixed rope.

"Clip on to that and drop over the edge. John will pull you across."

116

"Drop over the edge?" I said doubtfully.

"Yes," Bogel said. "Hurry up, man."

I tied into Timo's rope, clipped a sling onto the fixed line and the rope about my waist and felt for the edge with my foot. At that moment (it would have been a fine cinematic effect but it was no less real for that) the freshening wind thinned the clouds and sudden moonlight flashed down the great wall, illuminating the black, minutely crinkled jungle 2,600 feet below. I recoiled from the edge in dismay.

"Jesus, George!"

"Go on, Dave. It's okay."

Bogel's voice was tired and strained and I could see the rain glistening on his face. I turned to the abyss again and, screwing up my courage, jumped into it. I dropped six feet and felt the sickening stretch of the line as my weight came onto it. Then, like a bloodless, boneless duffel-bag, I was dragged across by Timo.

Once I hit the corner I felt a flood of elation. I scampered up the thirty feet of mire to the belay and began thumping Timo on the back. "What the hell made you jump across there, man! For God's sake!"

We leaned over to watch Bogel, who fell out at right angles to the wall and literally ran across it hauled violently by Straub, a horizontal sprinter on a vertical track. The sight was so extraordinary we burst into our first laugh of the day.

Twenty feet above the belay was a miserable little ledge with a sort of funnel in the rock overhead. This was our bivouac. The weepy moonlight filtered down to us and far above, giant beaks of rock marched upward into the swirling mist.

117

Groggy with exhaustion, we squeezed onto the ledge, hammered a couple of pitons into a crack and tied ourselves onto them in case we dozed off and rolled over the ledge. We crouched there, cramped and shivering.

"Tomorrow, John?" I asked.

"I don't know, Dave," Timo said, for he, like all of us, was now higher on the face than any man had ever been. "I don't know what's up there."

EIGHT

PINNACLITIS

Day Eight dawned in a thick drizzle. We looked at each other in the gray light and the signs of exhaustion were plain. We were gray too. We stood up and shook our cramped limbs, kneading our stiff fingers and shivering. The tiny ledge and the rock behind it were running with water. Our boots squelched as we shifted from one foot to the other. We had not taken them off for eight days, nor our ragged clothes either. None of us were in any condition for hard climbing.

Bogel stirred a powder into a mess-tin of rain-water and passed it around. Whatever it was, was white, lumpy and cold, but we forced it down because we knew it was all we would have to keep us going for maybe sixteen hours.

Timo was more silent than usual. He pulled a plastic envelope from the flap of his pack and took out a battered photograph. It was an aerial picture taken many years ago and showed part of the plateau and upper wall. Somewhere on it was the spot where we stood. After studying its blurred details a few minutes, he pushed it inside his shirt and slid down the fixed Tyrolean line to the level of last night's crossing. He wanted to compare the picture and the wall from a different angle.

We packed up, hammered out the pitons and were ready to go. Straub, the shivering optimist in a T-shirt, grinned at us. "Brace up, fellas. Just about 300 feet more and we'll be on top."

At that moment Timo pulled up over the edge, his face set. He held out the photograph. "This dark patch here looks like the Red Wall, right? In which case we're here on the left of the gray stretch above it. The overhangs above us are here on the picture. Do you agree?"

We looked from the photograph to the overhangs and back again, squinting at the fuzzy tones. Bogel glanced up the corner to our left and scored the picture with his thumbnail. ' "Here's the line of the corner. I think you're right."

Timo nodded and moved his finger up the picture. "Now look at this."

We leaned forward and saw a black, horizontal line an inch-and-a-half long. Straub jerked his head up. "My God! We're cut off! That's a god-almighty rift between us and the plateau!"

Our worst fear had become reality: We were on a pinnacle.

I

IN SIGHT OF THE TOP

We stood in stunned silence, and all at once we felt the accumulated weariness of the long struggle up the wall. Beaten now, after seven days? But in seconds our dejection changed to resentment, then anger. With the energy of rage we argued it out.

We had to *see* that rift. Suppose there was a boulder (or chockstone, as climbers call it) jammed across it, a chockstone the size of a house? Maybe we could get across it and up the far wall, which was a couple of hundred feet higher than our side. Or what if there was a solid spike of rock sticking out of the opposite wall? We'd damn well lasso it, fix the rope and swing across hand over hand. The chances of either solution were remote but we had to try.

Timo, the mud and grass maestro, attacked the last and steepest of the vegetation pitches and we followed. After 160 feet the pitch eased into a slope.

The sun grew stronger through thinning clouds. To the right a hundred-foot ledge ran straight across the same wall we had crossed by the Tyrolean farther down. It was as vertical as ever and we totted up the total exposure—2,750 feet straight down to the jungle. But above to the left, the grass slope ran comfortingly up into the hazy glow of the sun.

We moved up it quickly to where the rock rose again in weird towers, sculptured by the storms of thousands of years—We split up to search for a route, but there was nothing.

Retracing our way down the slope to the packs, we took stock. Timo pointed to the ledge on the right. "That's the only way we can go except down. We can cross it, dump everything in the first possible bivouac and get up to that rift. If there's a way across it we'll go straight for the top. If not, we've had it."

We roped up and traversed onto the ledge. For most of its length it was generous, but about twenty-five feet from the end it narrowed drastically where the upper wall bulged and forced us to lean out backward over the drop. Right there, in the worst possible spot, the ledge was blocked by a column of three squared-off boulders, five-and-a-half feet high. The top one wobbled but was too heavy to push off. In a way I was relieved, for I imagined it falling, down, down, until it became a minute speck and vanished, and still would have covered only a part of its long plunge.

Above the column the wall sloped sharply outward, and so did we as we climbed it. Six feet off the ground, or even fifty, we might have stepped around it with ease; 2,750 feet up, it was forbidding. Timo and Bogel somehow got the packs over and Straub and I followed.

Around the far corner of the ledge was a dry cave. There we dumped the packs, moved farther to the right and up a narrow, slimy gully to the base of three chimneys and a smooth, mossy wall. The chimney to the right seemed bottomless. That on the left was obviously the one to take and the man to take it was Bogel.

In fine style he mastered the chimney's thirty twisting feet and disappeared into a tunnel slanting upward through the huge boulders that formed its roof. Stones whizzed and cracked around us as he scrabbled up. Timo grabbed his head and cried out, stumbling against the wall. Seconds later, his face still screwed up with pain, he ascended the chimney himself. Straub, the packs and I followed in that order.

We emerged among a jumble of squat towers and boulders. It was the top of the pinnacle. Eighty feet in front of us a great wall rose 150 feet to a jagged rim.

"That's it," Timo said.

It was the plateau of the Auyán-Tepuí.

II

THE RIFT

Now that we could see the summit and knew how close it was, it was hard to believe we might not reach it. But that possibility was very real, for between it and us stretched the rift. Feverishly we coiled the ropes while Timo hurried off to reconnoiter. We were still at work when he came running and leaping back. He was waving his arms, stammering excitedly, "There's a chockstone! A *monster*!"

He turned and raced off again. We tore after him, up and over the boulders, around the towers, laughing like lunatics. As we reached the brink of the rift we saw it: our chockstone, the bridge that would take us off the pinnacle.

Twenty-five feet long by ten feet wide, and forty feet deep, the chockstone was jammed lengthwise across the eastern end of the rift, fifteen feet beneath us, a mere pebble wedged between two colossal walls, a pebble that could crush a locomotive flat, a pebble that geological chance had deposited there and without which we had no chance of crossing to the main face.

123

Its nearest neighbor was hundreds of feet below.

We rigged a fixed rope, lowered it and swarmed down. We looked along the rift to the right. Framed by its wet black walls was an immense face similar to the Angel's. It was the continuation northward of the Auyán-Tepuí, miles away, glowing red and yellow in the sun as it soared up out of the jungle. To the left, below, was the valley of the Churún River, bounded on the east by a wall parallel to ours. Beneath us, except for the chockstone, was nothing but air.

The view was not so picturesque as we studied the way up. A difficult wall rose 100 feet, and the only escape was a horizontal fault thirty feet up that ran leftward. The problem was how to reach it, and this we left to Bogel. He chose a groove slightly to the right of the chockstone, climbed it boldly to an overhang and moved left to a stance. There was no belay so he braced as firmly as he could and brought the three of us up.

But we still could not find a route to the top. Bearing left across a steep ledge, we attacked time and again. Each probe led to a dead end. We tried several cracks and chimneys, driving as hard as we could, only to find more walls and pinnacles beyond, looming and shifting in the gathering mist.

A narrow passage in the rock led down into a grotesque cave filled with bulges and niches, dripping noisily with water. In this dungeon, leaning breathless against the walls, we held a council.

"I don't believe it," Timo said. "As close as we are we're not going to make it today."

He was apologetic. "We should have been back four days ago. Paul and Dave have commitments and must have been given up for dead by now. If you feel we should go down, then we'll go down."

"Hell, no," we all said at once. "Let's give it another day."

"We'll have to cross that rift again," Timo said. "To go down for our packs. It'll take hours . . ."

I glanced at my watch. "My God, it's five o'clock! We only have one more hour of daylight!"

"I'll go down for the packs," Timo volunteered.

Straub would go with him while Bogel waited above the chockstone to bring them back up. I had no illusions about myself; the trip would crease me. I would station myself on the ledge and take the packs from Bogel as he hauled them up.

Operation Night Haul was underway.

III

OPERATION NIGHT HAUL

Timo and Straub descended to the chockstone, crossed it, scaled the wall on the other side and got down Bogel's Chimney in good time. At the bottom of the gully they sorted the essentials into two packs. Darkness caught them as they emerged from the chimney. With the flickering help of the ailing underwater flashlight, they groped back to the rift. Timo went down the fixed rope to the chockstone. Straub switched off the flashlight, clipped the packs on and shoved them over. Then he too eased his way down in total darkness. They both crawled across the chockstone to where Bogel was waiting above.

"If you switch that light on for just a second," Bogel said, "I'll drop the rope right onto you."

Timo caught the coils as they fell onto his shoulders.

"Remember," Bogel cautioned. "There's no belay here and I'm perched right over the face, so don't slip. I'll haul the packs one at a time, move them to Dave on the ledge and come back for you. There's only room up here for one man or one pack at a time. Okay?"

"Okay, George. First pack is on."

We could hear but not see the pack scraping up the rock. There was no belay on the chockstone either, and if Bogel fell he would drop sixty feet before the rope held him. As a precaution Timo handed it to Straub.

"Lie flat, Paul. If George peels off I'll drop over the edge on this side. That should hold him . . . unless the rope breaks."

But Bogel didn't fall. He took the first pack along that difficult traverse, feeling his way, handed it to me and returned for the second. Four journeys in the dark over a near-3,000-foot drop.

Three hours after the operation had started, as we were all moving back along the ledge, Straub just behind me, I said, "Paul, that must have been murder."

"Nothing to it, Dave," he said. "It was so dark I couldn't see the damn drop."

IV

LAST MEAL

There were bushy shrubs on the ledge and we collected them by the armful. Once in the cave we dug out the butane stove, jammed it up against the rock and hammered sparks into the escaping gas, for by now our matches were soaked and useless. All four of us crouched over the stove intently. We had to eat, we had to drive some of the cold from our bones, we had to cosset our remaining strength because, even after the summit, we still had the whole route to retrace, downward.

The descent would take two days to the foot of the wall and the best part of another to the base camp on the Churún River. If the Indians weren't there it would take maybe four days down the Churún and the Carrao to Canaima, providing we could construct some sort of raft. That made seven days. Now, in our ninth bivouac, we had two days' rations left, no matches and a half-empty butane tank.

When the stove whooshed into flame, we jumped about thumping each other, blinking in the light, laughing. Bogel and I got cracking on the chores. The dinner was sumptuous—mixed, cooked and eaten in the same pot. The fire was the biggest since the Blitz, roaring and crackling out of a blowhole in the roof. We steamed off, sipped our limeade tea and crept bone-tired under the soggy sleeping sack.

It was the last meal we were to have for three days and two nights.

LAST CHANCE

N I N E At first light I lifted the corner of the sop-blanket and peered up at a hundred-foot buttress of rock that rose to our left. It had the profile of a totem pole and its noses and beaks changed color from blurry gray to jet black as the rain and mist swept across them. My heart sank. It was the lousiest, soggiest weather of the whole climb, and on the very day, the final day, that should have been gold with sunlight.

This was our last chance to reach the summit. Once again we would leave everything behind except climbing equipment and make a dash for the plateau. We would not even carry food or water.

I

BEATEN

We crawled out from under the cover just as wet and a lot colder than we had been the night before. As I shuffled across the cave to the water container, I came to a halt, shocked. My legs were buckling. When I looked down at my feet,

my head swam. I reached for the wall to steady myself and glanced quickly to see if the others had noticed. They hadn't, and I forced myself outside into the rain. I was talking aloud: "Move along the ledge a bit. That's it. Now turn to face the rock. Brace up, idiot. Now try to climb. Just two or three feet. Step up just *one* move, can't you? Just one . . ."

I couldn't do it. Facing outward I eased my back down the wall until I was crouching on my heels. I tilted my face up into the rain.

"Why are you sitting there? Get up. You ill or something? You might get to the top today. Do you hear? The *top*."

But I wasn't thinking of the top. I was thinking of the sop-blanket. If I rolled up in it maybe I could get warm. Maybe my brain would stop swimming. Maybe I could sleep.

I rose to my knees and slowly pulled myself up. I felt no outrage, not even disillusion. Just the realization that if I was to have any chance at all of getting down the face, which would be the hardest part of the climb, I could not try for the summit. I was beaten. I went back down into the cave and told the others.

"You *what*? What's wrong?" said Timo.

"I've had it. I'm shaky. If I go on another day I'll have nothing left for the descent. It would be dangerous for you as well as for me."

"Come on, Dave. You'll make it. We'll give you a hand. It's only hours from the top. After eight days you *have* to go on now."

"No, John. I can't even walk around this cave without my legs folding. I'll stay behind and

pack up so we can move off right away when you get back."

They looked at me and at each other. Then Straub gave himself a sort of rousing shake: "David. You come on now. We'll *shove* you up. There's three of us."

I studied that bedraggled trio. They looked stooped and wan. They were busted too. I felt I was about to get either exasperated or wet around the eyes, so I ended the palaver abruptly, turning away and pulling out my tatty notebook and a stub of pencil.

"You'll need a message to leave on top if you get there. I'll write it in English and Spanish."

I scribbled hastily and read it out: "This paper was placed here by the first team to scale the East Wall of the Auyán-Tepuí, slightly right of the Angel Falls. The route took ten days climbing. The members of the team are: John Timo Jr., George Bogel, Dr. Paul Straub, David Nott."

We signed beside our names and added a note that the first two were members of the Pittsburgh Explorer's Club.

East Wall of the Auyán-Tepuí? We didn't even know where we were, for God's sake. Even Timo, who had lived and dreamed of the route for four years and had been on two previous expeditions, was so bone-weary, so totally absorbed in getting to the summit, that he failed to notice the mistake. The East Wall was miles away. We were on the West Wall of the Churún Gorge, which cuts into the Auyán-Tepuí from the north. Moreover, we had been on the wall eight days so far, not ten. This was the morning

131

of the ninth day. Later we were to realize these were not my only errors.

II

A CALL FROM SOMEWHERE

I handed the note to Timo and watched somberly as the three left the cave and traversed back in the direction of the chockstone, but at a higher level. Once alone I stood for some time, thinking things over and getting nowhere. My notion of creeping back under the wet sleeping sack faded in disgust. I couldn't face the soggy, muddy feel of it, nor the squelch of the ground beneath it. So I packed everything and sat beside the fire's ashes to wait.

Seeping rain fell from the different levels of the roof, plumping and pattering on the floor, tinkling in the pools of water, splatting on the rocks. I had just about worked out the various rhythms of this demented drumming when I thought I heard a call from somewhere above. Shuffling stiffly out of the cave, I shouted, "Say again!"

There was no answer in the sound-deadening mist.

"Where are you?"

Again no answer.

I stood outside maybe a quarter-of-an-hour, staring dully at the rain, when suddenly I heard Timo calling out: "Dave. Are you coming?"

His voice was startlingly clear through the

clouds and drizzle. I felt a pulse of excitement and jumped down into the cave, grabbed my slings and karabiners, got back out and stumbled along the slope at the foot of the ramparts, in the direction of Timo's voice, yelling "Yes!" and "Hold on!" and "Bloody Good!" I found him grinning at the top of an easy chimney. I nipped up quickly, grinning myself.

"Dammit! That's better! I'd never forgive myself for staying down there!"

I felt very grateful. But it was difficult to know whom to be grateful to. Providence, I guess. Because we still don't know who called first. Timo says he heard me shout and, thinking I was on my way to join them, came back to the top of the chimney to guide me up.

Probably the first voice I heard had been a call between themselves. It might have been Bogel sounding off at someone or something. But whatever it was, I was on my way, astonished at my lifting spirits and more so at my legs, which were trundling me along a higher ledge toward the final wall of rock. My knees were bent and creaking a bit, but I was moving, by God, and about to enter some of the weirdest terrain on earth: the Labyrinth.

III

THE LABYRINTH

The last couple of hundred feet to the top of the face of Angel Falls are more a cluster of

towers than a continuous wall. Over the ages,
streams from millions of tons of tropical rain
have cut deep channels into the edge of the plateau. The falls itself shoots out from one such
gorge 200 feet below the summit. These gorges
are almost as immense and far more complex
than the skyscraper canyons of Manhattan. This
was the maze we were about to penetrate.

Before us the wall was split by a narrow cleft
two feet wide and sixty feet high. We followed
this forbidding passageway for several yards
until it opened dramatically into a sort of moon
crater scooped out of the plateau and cradling a
crumbling ruin of stone. It was like bursting into
the internal intricacies of a medieval castle
through an underground tunnel. We had got in
at the base of its front wall. We wanted to get
out at the top of its rear wall, for up there was
the flat plateau of the tableland mountain.

We could not believe our eyes. Everywhere we
looked there were pinnacles, corners, angles,
cracks, walls and overhangs, all rising perhaps
sixty feet from our level and, as we soon discovered, all dropping to unknown depths below. It
was like traversing within the crevasses of an Ice
Age glacier or through some fearfully deep and
complicated cave from which the roof had been
lifted. Moreover, in the Labyrinth, wherever
there was a nook or cranny, we found earth or
mud in which grew plants fit for a madman's
window-box, a vegetable world undisturbed in
all history by any man or animal: plants two
feet high and two feet wide clinging to a half-
inch of dripping dirt; plants whose roots twined
up their own stems; mosses we sank into up to

134

the knee; and here and there, incredibly out of place, a pale palm tree, straight and slim.

Our own course was unplottable: twenty feet up, three across, thirty down, ten to the right, double back through a tunnel, around a ledge. Every step had to be taken with extreme care, for these giant, jumbled boulders, slabs and blocks had never felt the weight of anything but insect life, and we feared that at any moment the balance of geological ages would be disturbed by our intrusion and the whole structure would collapse, grinding us to nothing in its thunderous fall. We kept glancing up, trying to memorize the main features of the rim of rock above so we could find our way back. Through all the passages of the maze blew a thick drizzling mist. If this was the Lost World, it was far older than that of Conan Doyle's fiction; here, the dinosaurs were millions of years in the future, and we, the first men, were aeons out of our time.

This fanciful notion gave way to a concrete problem. There was a forty-foot-high wall blocking our passage through the maze. On climbing it, however, we found it was not a wall but the tip of a colossal chockstone jammed across a great rift, the Number Two gully, which had repulsed us below. Up to now the chockstones in the maze had been so thickly clustered we had thought we were in a corridor with a floor. Now we saw we were once again on a huge boulder with nothing beneath it but air.

The other side of this boulder sloped down to a gap ten feet wide. Across the gap was another chockstone that sloped up thirty feet.

"My God," said Straub. "That gap drops through into the rift. That's more than 1,000 feet deep!"

So far only Bogel had fallen into a hellhole. Now it was my turn. Timo took a few coils of rope in his hand, skidded down the slippery rock, leaped across the gap and scrabbled up the slope of the second chockstone as if the devil were after him. An extraordinary performance.

I was next. I had a rope from Timo and one from Bogel. I slid cautiously down the latter to the edge and peered into the rift. It was an appalling drop and sapped the nerve I needed to make the leap across. Instead I moved a few yards to the right, where the gap narrowed. Here I could jump across to a small ledge and then climb up.

I was giving the knots at my waist a final check when I slipped on the wet rock. Cartwheeling over the edge I plunged headfirst into the rift, glimpsing a whirling patch of sky above my boots. My head hit the rock with a bang as I went through the gap, then the ropes stopped me with a jerk. But I was below the chockstones, unable to reach the rock on either side. I swung back and forth over that drop like a sky-diver beneath his parachute. As I pendulumed I heard the ropes rasping on the edge of the chockstones.

My head cleared and I shouted frantically to Bogel to slack off. He did so and I swung across to the other side, where Timo hauled me until I could pull up onto the ledge and climb to him.

"You okay, Dave?" he asked.

I nodded, trembling.

We brought the others across. There was no time for sympathy, nor even a sly crack from Bogel. Beyond the second chockstone we could see that the maze continued as difficult and complex as ever.

IV

"YOU FIRST, JOHN"

Again I felt a twinge of panic and disbelief. The summit might be no more than fifty feet above. But had we chosen the wrong line up to it? Would we ever find the right line in this confusion?

Timo seemed to sense what was on our minds. "We can't backtrack now," he said. "It's this route or nothing. But let's get out of this rift."

He pointed to a slippery finger-crack cutting up an overhanging wall. There was not a hold on it for twelve feet. "Quick, Paul," he said. "Brace yourself at the bottom there."

Timo climbed from the doctor's knee to his shoulder, then to his head and, amazingly, up onto his hand, held straight up. Straub was shaking from the strain and clearly couldn't hold him a second longer. Timo fought his way up, slipped, recovered and flung himself up onto a ledge.

"Beautiful! Beautiful!" Bogel yelled. We whooped and applauded.

Straub shoved me up as far as he could, Timo heaved me the rest of the way and we hauled the

137

others up on the rope. We traversed along the
ledge, stooping under an overhang, turned a
corner and found ourselves at the bottom of a
crevasse. But this time its walls were only twenty-five feet high and above them we could see
the open sky. To our left the crevasse was
jammed with huge greasy boulders rising in steps
toward the rim.

"That's got to be the plateau!" Straub cried.

"Don't count on it," warned Timo. "There
may be another series of walls above this."

We moved carefully up the boulders, glancing
down at the deep drop between them. With every move upward the light grew brighter. There
was a new freshness in the air. Above the last
boulder, in the last eight feet of the crevasse, a
rickety tree sprouted from a crack.

I turned to Timo with suppressed excitement.
"You first, John. You never know . . ."

He climbed up and over the edge, looked
around briefly, leaned down to us and said,

"Gentlemen, this is the top."

V

THE LOST WORLD

The Auyán-Tepuí plateau at this point was
flat, black, slippery rock dotted with rainpools
and boulders, split by deep crevasses. We could
see only thirty yards in the churning clouds and
here and there weird towers and blocks loomed
and shifted as the mist moved across them. It

138

was utter desolation. If astronauts were to land on the moon in a heavy drizzle, this is what they would see.

We crossed two crevasses with immense care, for it was like walking on ice, and suddenly we were on grass—thick mountain turf, flat and soft. Timo gave a whoop and ran around in a little circle. Then we were all skittering about. We had been nine days and eight nights on a vertical wall where not a single step could be taken without thought. Now we dodged this way and that, played tag, jumped sideways and backward.

Our jig of freedom became a dance of triumph. We waltzed around in a four-man bear-hug, slapping and punching each other.

"We did it!"

"We're up!"

"We got it!"

"Wha-ha!"

More quietly we shook Timo's hand and said, "Congratulations, John."

We had two tasks to complete before we began the descent. The first was to cross to the 200-foot-deep gorge through which the Angel River runs before dropping over the face to form the falls. It would be dangerous to lose our way here; in the mist we might never find our route down again. So we moved thirty yards leftward, stopping at a point from which the entrance to the Labyrinth was still in sight. Here I stayed while the others went on, leaving one man at each limit of visibility until Timo went on alone toward the edge of the gorge. He was looking for the aluminum tube in which the 1968 expedition had left a record of its visit; he wanted to add our ascent to it. But in the thick clouds he never found it.

In fifteen minutes we were all back at the entrance to the Labyrinth and the next job was to build a cairn of stones to mark the spot. I found a black and green rock fourteen inches long. One crack with a piton hammer split it cleanly across the middle. Inside, it was a lovely pale pink. This was the base of an eighteen-inch pile we erected on a boulder and under which we put an aluminum 35 mm. film container holding the message I had written that morning.

Before we put it in, we noticed I had dated it January 13, 1970, instead of 1971. We stared at it in bewilderment. In a small way this was a matter of history and the pencil stub was down in the bivouac. Finally Bogel exploded, "What the hell! Everybody writes the wrong year for a couple of weeks after January 1. And anyway, we've spent the whole of what's gone of the year on the trail. We've never had to write 1971 before."

We screwed the cap on and fitted the container into the cairn.

It was the moment for pictures. Straub and Timo balanced their cameras on a boulder with delayed-action springs set and scuttled across the rock to get all four of us in the shot. Out came the flag of the Pittsburgh Explorer's Club, and, in miniature, the Stars and Stripes, and the yellow, blue and red banner of Venezuela.

"I have a surprise for you, David," Timo said, and he pulled out a Union Jack, five-and-a-half inches by four. I'd never been so taken with a gesture in all my life. I really was most absurdly pleased.

So there we stood, four dripping, mud-soaked tramps, close to exhaustion, holding up our little wet flags and beaming self-consciously at the cameras as they clicked off pictures like robots. No one in the whole world knew where we were, and all we could see was mist.

Part **III**

THE
DESCENT

THE
HARD WAY DOWN

TEN

A shriek of laughter came across the abyss. "Yes, there you are, you English dog, and there you will remain! I have waited and waited, and now has come my chance. You found it hard to get up; you will find it harder to get down. You cursed fools, you are trapped, every one of you!"

—from *The Lost World*

The summit scene was doleful and soon our spirits sank to suit it. We had made it, but now in our weakened state we faced the unquestionably greater risks of the descent.

Nobody has ever climbed down the north face of the Matterhorn or the Eiger or any other route of similar severity. If you get up this sort of route alive you get off the mountain as fast as you can, the easiest way available. Of course, the wall of Angel Falls was no Alpine north face. There were no blizzards or ice to contend with. But 3,282 feet was 3,282 feet whatever the latitude and the only other way off the plateau was a two-week march south or west, which we had no rations for. Expedition funds did not run to airdrops of food; all we had to keep us alive we carried on our backs.

145

Descent is more difficult and dangerous than ascent because on vertical or overhanging rock you cannot see the route below you. But there is a technique for sliding down such rock on a rope called rappelling. First the rope is hitched over a belay and its two ends thrown down the cliff. You pass the rope through a karabiner attached to a figure-eight loop of rope in which you sit. Then you step backward off your stance and walk down the cliff, controlling your descent by the friction of the rope running through the karabiner and over your shoulder. You should be protected by a safety rope tied around your waist and paid out by the man above, who can hold you if the rappel rope or belay breaks. The most experienced climber comes last and without this protection.

Rappelling may be required for descending rock towers on a saw-tooth ridge or escaping from a cliff in such emergencies as a sudden storm. Some climbers do it for kicks, and it is indeed an exhilarating and sometimes sensational maneuver. But few ever try it for 3,282 feet and two days.

Retracing our route through the Labyrinth and down to our last bivouac, we paused to work out tactics. We had little food and no matches, so it was essential to get off the wall quickly.

"We can tie the 200-foot and the 150-foot ropes together," said Timo. "If we're lucky with belays we can drop 170 feet each rappel."

"That means no safety rope—the third rope is only 120 feet long," I said. "If the belay or rappel rope breaks we don't stand a chance."

Bogel looked up from fiddling with the packs, mustache flaring, the raw flesh glistening red in the gashes in his shaved scalp. "For God's sake. We go down without a safety rope. Quit worrying about your damn insurance."

"It's the only way, Dave," Timo insisted. "We have to move fast."

I noticed Straub was peculiarly attentive to the discussion, his face getting longer by the minute. If he had spoken up about what was bothering him, we would have changed our plans entirely. But he said nothing. So the decision was made: We would rappel without protection.

I

STRAUB'S SECRET

Reversing the Night Haul we got across the rift and down Bogel's Chimney and the gully below. We were moving fast enough, as it turned out, to become careless. Careless enough to bring about the worst kit loss of the whole climb.

One by one we crossed the difficult ledge with the wobbly blocks and climbed down the 160-foot corner to the Tyrolean Traverse. Bogel went first across the fixed line and I followed, looking anywhere but downward, to join him on the triangular ledge.

"If you rig a rappel rope you can start down the chimney while I bring the others across," Bogel suggested.

"What rope?"

"The damn 120-foot rope. What the hell else?"

"I haven't got the bloody rope. It's up where Paul belayed me when I came down the corner."

"You mean you *left* it there?"

"I didn't leave it anywhere. I was down first, remember? You three ferried the kit down."

Bogel and I glowered at each other. But we both knew that squabbles on a climb are lethal, so we shut up. We were all at fault, and this was a serious mistake. In the event of an accident, that third rope would be vital. As it was now, we no longer had a safety rope.

Straub, moreover, was about to let me in on his secret. He came swinging across the fixed line and we rigged his rope to hang down the 100-foot chimney. Slipping into his thigh loops and clipping the rope through the karabiner, he leaned close to me conspiratorially and whispered, "Which shoulder does it go over?"

I gaped at him. "You don't *know*, Paul? You said you hadn't climbed before but John thought you'd rappelled on a practice rock somewhere."

"Well, I haven't. Quick, show me."

Aghast, I looked over the edge. "You can't *start* with that pitch, man. Not without a safety rope. You'll kill yourself."

His voice hissed in my ear. "Dave, there's nothing we can do about it. Come on. Show me."

Cursing, I put the rope over his left shoulder and into his right hand behind him. "Control it with *that* hand," I said, "and lean right out when you go over the edge."

He nodded and stepped backward into space. I watched as he went straight down at a steady, controlled speed. It was a perfect rappel.

II

LUCKY ESCAPES

The doctor survived this pitch because of his inborn physical skill. Bogel, an expert, was to survive by sheer luck.

As the ropes had to be retrieved, the last man down would have to tie the two together and suspend them by a sling through which they could be hauled down after his descent. Since there was no other belay, however, the sling had to be hitched over the sharp-edged block above the chimney, which could cut through it. Unfortunately the only sling we could spare was my remaining prusik loop, made of nylon cord a mere five-sixteenths of an inch thick. The last man's nerves would have to be a darn sight stronger than his belay. Bogel volunteered to take the risk and Timo and I went ahead to hold one end of the joined ropes at the bottom while he rappelled down the other.

Bogel descended slowly, trying to avoid any sharp movement that might wear the sling through on the edge of the block. As he landed safely, we slapped him on the back, then turned to haul the rope down. The first jerk brought it tumbling the full hundred feet about our ears. The sling had been worn to a single strand; and a single pull had cut it.

Timo was next on the list of lucky escapes. The clouds were gathering again and as we pushed down past the rock-toothed bivouac a full Auyán-Tepuí storm enveloped us. The wind swept across the wall, whistling and booming among the crags and driving sheets of stinging rain in our faces. In minutes the rock, the ropes and ourselves were streaming with water.

Bogel took the lead and vanished down into the mist. Following him, I eased down a chimney to the edge of a long drop and perched there a moment with my face turned out of the wind. From 150 feet below, Bogel shouted, "Get your asses down here fast or we'll be caught by the dark! We can't stay on this ledge. No shelter!"

The message barely reached me through the storm, but it was clear Bogel was alarmed. I had to rappel the height of a fifteen-story building to a mean ledge and I glanced at the piton supporting the mud-soaked ropes. Old and rusted, a leftover from the expedition of two years ago, it was badly placed in a horizontal crack at the bottom of a bulge, and I realized with a stab of panic that a sharp downward pull could split the rock. I looked around for an alternative belay but there was nothing.

I worked it out fast. If the rock splits, I get killed. If the piton pulls out, I get killed. If the rope breaks, I get killed. Unless all three hold I'll end up a seeping bag of bone-bits. But if I hang around any longer we'll be caught by darkness. We are exhausted and another night on this wall without shelter will wreck us.

Bogel's voice rose again through the mist:

"*Go*, man! Quit worrying about your goddamn neck!"

I grimaced at the piton. "Stay put, you bastard," I muttered and, nerves cringing, backed over the edge in the swiftly fading light, down the dripping rope, thirty, forty, seventy feet, lurching in space under an overhang, swinging back hard against the wet, black rock (Lord, keep that piton in!), down again, ninety, 120 feet, on down with the rain streaming in my face and the rope burning through my hands, until I landed, a breathless, thankful heap on the ledge below.

Timo's voice sounded immediately from above: "Packs on!"

We watched them hurtling toward us and, as each came within ten feet of our heads, we jerked the rope out from the face to brake them. This was violent work; I pictured the piton grating and shifting in its crack at each wrench. And there were still two of us to come.

"Packs down! Come on!" I yelled.

It was Straub's turn. I winced as he backed over the edge and put his weight on the rope. Then down he plunged, straight over the overhang and down again, to thud at last onto the ledge. There was one more to go.

Timo showed way up in the clouds, leaning out on the rope. He kicked off boldly and came barreling toward our upturned faces, eighty, 130 feet, closer and closer. Then, just as he touched, a splintering crack rang out above us and we ducked against the wall. Coiling and thrashing, the heavy rope swished down; stone fragments thumped around us and we heard the clink of a falling piton through the howling wind. The rock had split.

III

THE DEVIL MOUNTAIN TOBOGGAN

It was already night: the fourth time darkness had caught us climbing. Three times before, we had conducted tricky night operations and slept reasonably safely, if not soundly. But now we were to be treated to a free ride on the Devil Mountain Toboggan.

We stood shaking on that miserable ledge scarcely able to stammer through our chattering teeth. We accepted the fact there would be no food or shelter and little sleep. But what we could not see was that the ledge sloped steeply outward, more steeply than we could cope with in the dark.

We felt around for the packs, dragged out the soaked sleeping sack and crouched under it to escape the wind, Timo beside us wrapped in his hammock. Then the mountain made its first move. Without warning, the layer of mud on the rock beneath us broke away and we were sliding rapidly down to the edge: our first ride of the night. Throwing off the sleeping sack, we clawed at the rock and scrabbled back up the slope.

"Everyone still here?" Timo gasped. "Dave? Paul? George?"

We grunted in reply and Straub felt around

below us. "Quick," he said. "Where's that sack? Get under it. We've got to preserve any warmth we can."

We retrieved the cover and huddled under it, bracing ourselves as best we could at the back of the ledge. But with each momentary surrender to exhaustion we would wake to find ourselves on the Toboggan again, slithering down to a drop we couldn't see. The free rides continued for ten hours and the rain fell ceaselessly until water was streaming down the wall onto our heads and cascading over the ledge beneath us.

At 5:30 next morning, in the first hint of light, we decided to run for it. Dizzy with fatigue, plastered with mud, we stood up in the hammering rain. We still had more than 2,000 feet to go.

IV
THE BATTLE OF THE TREES

Next came the Battle of the Trees. Descending from the ledge, we traversed right, rappelled down Timo's Chimney, passed through our bivouac of six nights ago and paused above a sweeping wall that dropped 150 feet with a fifty-foot chimney below it and, below that, a fifty-foot overhanging chockstone pitch dropping to a split-level cave.

Simple. Except for the trees.

At several points on the wall there were shrubs in the crannies, and here and there a tree clung to where some lunatic wind had lifted its seed. These trees had sprouted in some barely adequate crevice and, as they had grown, sent feelers across the rock in search of earth. Some had up to five main roots running in as many directions, burrowing into cracks. Some were solid enough for a belay, others too precarious to touch. By mischance three of them were growing in a direct line beneath the only rappel belay we could find.

Bogel lifted a handful of coils from the 200-foot rope, making sure those at his feet would run free, swung them back and forth on his slippery stance and heaved them over the edge. "Damn!" The rope had caught in the first tree, and he wearily hauled it back. Again and again he heaved the rope, cursed, hauled it back and recoiled it for a fresh throw.

"Those damn trees," he gasped.

"Let the rope hang there, George," said Timo at last, stepping up to the belay.

Clipping onto the rope, he rappelled down, stopping twelve feet above the first tree. Then he kicked out from the wall, dropped like a stone and crashed through the tree in an explosion of branches and leaves. On he went, straight through the next and the next with the debris fluttering down around him and the waterdrops flying. On a sunny day on some domesticated cliff this might have been funny. Here, after nine days on the wall, forty-two hours without food, each plunge made my nerves jump. But Timo had cleared the way.

We followed him to the bottom of the wall, rigged the next rappel and made it down to our bivouac of seven nights before. I had already thought about Timo's parka. We were approaching the spot where, carelessly, unforgivably, Straub and I had left it behind a week ago. More than once during the days of drenching rain I had watched Timo shivering and had cursed myself.

We were at the top of a twenty-foot wall. "Well," I said to Timo wryly, "at least you'll have your parka when we get down this."

He nodded his rain-slicked head.

Sure enough, when we reached the bottom, there it was, bright blue in the muddy grass. Timo grabbed it with relief. It was the one lost item the Angel had not swallowed for good.

Swallow it couldn't but snicker it could. Traversing a long southward ledge we suddenly became aware of something different; some fundamental fact of life had changed. Timo, clutching his precious waterproof parka, a piece of equipment that could have saved him days of misery, looked up and sniffed the air.

"Gentlemen," he said, "it's stopped raining."

V

READY-MIX RECOVERY

We sprawled on the ledge, oblivious to everything but the blessed absence of pounding rain. Rain that had drenched us for twenty hours, pursuing us down the face, smearing the cracks and chimneys with slime. Soon the clouds cleared and, far below, was the winding Churún, the green jungle and, rising from it, the yellow and pink east wall of the valley. We could make out the junction of the Churún and Angel rivers, which was the site of our base camp. But no matter how we squinted we were too high up to see whether our Indian crew was still there.

We had asked them to wait five days to take us back to Camarata, but we had underestimated the Angel. The five days had already stretched into nine. Surely the Indians' food had run out, as ours had. What would we do if they had gone?

"We cut a log each and run the rapids on them," said Straub. "When we get to the Carrao we turn west downstream instead of upstream to Camarata. In two or three days we could float down to Canaima."

We listened spellbound. He was our river expert and his plan was bold and beautiful.

"But we got nothing to cut the logs with, Paul," said Bogel.

"And no rations."

"And I bet one of us can't swim."

Anyway, we had more than 1,000 feet of wall to get down first. We'd worry tomorrow about starving in the jungle or drowning in the rapids. Right now we were concerned with battered ropes and insecure pitons. The Indians would either be there or, God forbid, they wouldn't.

Struggling to his feet, Timo reminded us there was a water spring on the ledge. I turned to my pack to get the canteen out. It was a simple operation: unfasten two straps, untie the cord and rummage about inside. But it took me five minutes. I couldn't close my swollen hands enough to grasp the straps and had to shove my fingers up to my thumb with my knee. My forearms were bunched in a tight cramp. I knew that when we went over the edge for the next pitch my hands would close tight on the rope: the drop below would see to that. But could I keep them there even though, with no safety rope, the alternative was to become an unidentifiable blob hundreds of feet below?

I was on the point of insisting on staying put on the ledge until my arms uncramped. It's my life, I thought, what the hell does a couple of hours' delay matter? But as I turned to the others, Timo produced a powder from our rations. Mixing it in a water bottle, he tasted the brew and announced Instant Orange Breakfast Juice. We sipped it as if it were a vintage claret and its sugar ran through us like a magic potion. The drink so revitalized us we felt ready for anything. On our next rappel we would learn how wrong we were.

VI

THE END OF OUR ROPE

The first victim was me. Somewhere down the line, dropping over an overhang, I landed astride the taut belay rope and it caught me hard in the groin. Gasping with pain, I fell off it to the left and swung back under the overhang, my hip and shoulder crashing into the rock.

Now I found the free end of my rappel rope had snagged in a tree above and I was stuck. Feet flat against the rock, right hand clinging to the rope, I strove to jerk the end loose with my left. What I had long feared suddenly happened: My hands opened up. Desperately I twisted my arm around the rope and dropped. With a rasping crack the snagged line broke free, its coils burning around my arm, and as the friction slowed me I grabbed for the loose end and regained control.

Fifty feet farther I reached a ledge. I had to force my fingers off the rope with the heel of my other hand and squat with both hands behind my knees to stop shaking. Slumped there, cursing between gasps, I realized I wasn't angry but querulous. I sounded like some sick old man mumbling his complaints.

I got up and crawled down a gully toward Timo, who was sitting, head on his knees, on the edge of a steep corner. Together we waited for the other two. For a while we said nothing, a very long while. Then: "There must be something wrong up there."

"Yes, I guess so."

It was all the reaction we were capable of. Getting to our feet and climbing back up the gully, we saw Straub rappelling fifty feet up just above the overhang. He was the second victim.

As he kicked off from the wall to drop under the overhang, he failed to brake himself and plummeted straight down. Helplessly we

158

watched him fall twenty-five feet, hit a ledge and bounce off. But in this split-second halt he managed to pull the rope tight across his back and stop the plunge. He reached us under control, pale but grinning. "That rope's so damn slippery I even tried to stop myself with my teeth."

Victim number three endured a more subtle penance. As we hauled the rope down it caught firmly in a groove it had worn in the belay tree. One of us would have to climb back up to free it. He would have to go more than 150 feet up those overhanging chimneys and cracks to yank it loose and rig it higher in the tree to begin the descent again.

I'm ashamed to say I became engrossed in relacing my boots until I heard some brave soul volunteer for the job. It was Bogel. An hour later he came back into view, down the overhang and the last fifty feet to join us. He said nothing. Not a word of complaint.

While Timo went ahead to find the next belay, the rest of us sorted and coiled the ropes and dragged them and the packs across a long ledge—"dragged" is the word. We were slowing visibly, and when we stumbled we stayed down for those telling extra seconds, like a prizefighter on his third knock-down. Trailing behind, I watched Bogel and Straub, who had hauled hundreds of pounds up the wall with snap and swagger, now jerking the packs along painfully, out of rhythm, a couple of feet at a time. Moments later, as dead as we were, we would all be howling and hooting with more energy than we could spare.

VII

"KEEP THE BOMB!"

On the next rappel, I had just reached Timo and Bogel on a small ledge and Straub was starting down toward us when we heard a plane. We scanned the sky and, high above, we spotted the Radio Caracas Cessna. For eight days, despite the pilot's daredevil flying, the clouds had prevented them from sighting us and we had been unable even to get the radio out to make contact. This time Bogel got through to them instantly and guided the pilot down to our altitude.

They'll get their film at last, we thought. But they still couldn't find us, even though the plane zoomed right in, banking away at the last moment to avoid smashing into the wall.

They were frantic. "For God's sake, fellows!" cried the pilot. "Explode the bomb!"

He was referring to the big smoke-bomb we had been given as a distress signal.

"Explode the bomb! The smoke will show where you are! It will be a sensational film!"

Sure it would. We would like to see that film ourselves. But we had other plans for that bomb. Somewhere, somehow, we were going to light a fire with it. A *fire*. Something to heat up the mud we had to sleep in or at least make a hot drink before the night clammily enfolded us. We *needed* that smoke-bomb.

We sounded like some upside-down peace rally.

160

"Keep the bomb!" we yelled to Bogel. "Save the bomb! We want the bomb, George!"

In exasperation Bogel flapped his hand behind his back to quiet us as he crouched over his radio and spoke placatingly into the hand-set: "Oh, yes, fellows, the bomb. Well . . . it went over the edge, fellows. Yes, lost it. Sorry, boys."

"Keep the bomb!" we were yelling. "Save the bomb!"

Bogel's ferocious face whipped around at us, writhing like that of the villain in the Chaplin movies, mouthing imprecations, eyebrows and mustachios wiggling.

"Shut up, you bums!" he roared and, whipping back to his microphone, became lamblike again: "No, fellows, I'm afraid we have no flares either. We . . . we haven't even got any *matches*."

His tone was so forlorn we almost fell 500 feet laughing, and the Cessna, deprived of its fireworks, buzzed away at last without a picture.

VIII

'ONE MORE TO GO'

Continuing down to the last main ledge of the wall, we traversed right in search of a belay point. We had to be especially careful with this one, because the only stopping place on the 300-foot drop was the narrow ledge where we had bivouaced the first night. It was hidden from us by 100 feet of overhangs and we had to locate the exact spot or the first man down would reach the end of the rope to find himself hanging over nothing.

We rigged a belay with nylon webbing and a karabiner. Timo went over the edge and I followed. The rappel was airy in the extreme, dropping over big overhangs, one after another. It should have been exhilarating. For me, expecting my grip to loosen any second, it was misery and I landed cursing at the pain in my arms.

Timo looked across at me. "One more to go, Dave," he said. I glanced down and saw the jungle sloping to the river three miles away, the topmost trees a mere 150 feet below. In retrospect his next remark was reckless: "We're almost there. We can't let anything go wrong now. No accidents."

Amen, I thought, peering down. It was like standing on a window ledge fourteen stories up.

"We've only got forty-five minutes before dark," I said. "We better hurry."

The sun had already set and shadows were creeping up the valley by the time we got the packs down and the rappel rigged. Timo went first, disappearing below an overhang, then called to say the rope did not reach the bottom. "Give me all the slack you've got," he shouted.

We were rerigging when suddenly the rope jerked out of our hands and ran violently out over the belay.

"My God, he's fallen!" Bogel cried.

Straub grabbed his medical kit: "Quick. Secure the rope and I'll go first."

There was no time for belaying. Bogel and I

162

gripped the rope and braced ourselves, and the doctor went over the edge. By now it was almost night. As soon as Straub was down we rigged a running belay and clipped the ropes into it. I went next and found him at the bottom.

"John fell about thirty feet and may have a fracture of some sort in his arm," he said. "I want to examine him as soon as we get on firm ground."

"But where the hell *is* he!" I said glancing around.

"He's gone on to look for a bivouac site and asks if someone will take his pack."

"Well, gawd stone the bleeding crows!" I breathed.

I grabbed the pack and tore off, stumbling along the foot of the face, up and over the boulders, down and up the gullies, through the damned tearing undergrowth, until Timo's voice, calm as ever, brought me up short in the dark.

"It's up here, Dave. Over to your left a bit."

Scrambling up to him, I laid an accusing finger on his chest: "What's the big idea, Timo? We're trying to get everyone down alive and you mess it up. Paul's going to amputate at base camp before you start swimming down the rapids."

He stood shivering in the small clearing, holding his arm tight against his body. Above us the tall trees were rustling. Beneath our feet was solid earth.

"We're down, John," I said quietly.

"Yes."

"And we're all in one piece."

"Yes," Timo said.

ELEVEN

NO MORE VERTICAL

It was full night by now and I went back to guide the others in. Some guide! I couldn't even find my own way. First, the forest was a thick, tangled, prickly, fleshy-leaved jungle. Second, the terrain was a nightmare maze of giant boulders that had tumbled from the face over the ages and now sat strangled by the creeping green. Third, I was wobbly on my pins and shaking from something or other—maybe laughter.

Whatever it was, there was a large shot of relief in it. Nothing mattered now. We could starve, we could drown in the rapids, we could die of exhaustion and exposure in the jungle, but we didn't have to stare into the abyss anymore. No more launching ourselves over the sickening drop on an unsafe belay without a damn thing to do about it if that sudden lurching, rushing fall comes. No more vertical . . .

"Goddamn jungle! Where the hell *are* you guys?

I jumped at the voice. It was Bogel roaring again, three feet from my ear in the darkness.

"We're over here, George," I whispered. "About 500 yards to your right."

He let out a satisfying squawk of fright, but

Straub quickly cut off the horseplay: "Let's get back to John. I want a proper look at his arm."

We stumbled to the clearing, and there Bogel and I listened tensely as Straub questioned Timo in his quiet voice: "Does it hurt here? And here? Now let's bend it slowly . . ."

Timo answered in monosyllables—yes, no, uh-huh—and with gasps of pain. In the darkness I reached out to touch him; I wanted to know where he was so I would not bump against him. It was an eerie moment—a doctor's inquiring voice evocative of bright lights and instruments, white tiles and linen—here in this black jungle with the great wall above us.

"I'd say there's no fracture, John," Straub announced at last. "Perhaps a bone chip. But you can't use that arm. I'll strap you up and you'll have to go easy on the way down tomorrow."

That was it. You might call it the worst of bad luck to fall the last thirty feet of a 3,000-foot wall. You might call it the best of good luck that it was the *last* thirty feet.

I

TO BUILD A FIRE

"John needs something hot to eat or at least to drink," Straub said. "We all do. We've got to get a fire going."

There was a chance of starting a fire with the smoke-bomb, but we needed kindling and wood. We had no water, but there would be some in

166

the ripped plastic container we had left at the first bivouac site along the base of the wall to the left. Someone had to get it.

"That's more than difficult. It's dangerous," said Timo. "You can get lost out there or break an ankle. I think we'll have to do without water."

While we were talking, and on the remotest chance, I dug out my flashlight, which had given up the ghost after the Night Haul. I shook it and banged it on my boot and suddenly it lit!

"That's beautiful!"

"Terrific!"

"Now we can get the water!"

"Maybe we can get to eat something!"

The flashlight went out. I shook it and it lit again, flickered, then failed. I banged it again and it lit again. Straub put his hand on my wrist: "Switch it off, Dave. Save it. I'll go for the water with it and if you get a fire going at least I'll have a sort of beacon to guide me back."

I handed him the flashlight. "Well, Paul, I'm bloody glad it's you and not me."

While Straub fixed Timo up, Bogel and I fumbled about for wood and kindling, no mean task in that lousy, sopping jungle. We estimated we had fifteen minutes of gas in our butane camping stove and we tried to light it by striking sparks from a stone with a piton hammer. It didn't work. There was nothing for it but the bomb.

We fished it out and passed it around in the dark. It was heavy and sinister and made my flesh crawl to handle it. Nobody admitted as much, but now that the moment to use it had

167

arrived we were nervous. We couldn't see the instructions and I had to thrust out of my mind the image of burned and blasted faces and hands. It was like a big grenade with a pin and a release lever. Pull the pin, release the lever and get the hell out of the way. Instead we had to get in close with the butane stove to catch the initial detonation.

Decisively, Straub pulled the pin, dropped the bomb and we all crouched around it, Bogel with the hissing stove, Straub and I with the soaked matches and a handful of twigs. The bomb went off with a crack, a whoosh of sparks and dense clouds of smoke. Choking and gasping, we lay next to it, spluttering curses until Straub, burning his fingers, managed to get a match in and drew it out lit. Bogel shoved his stove close and we leaped away with delight as it caught and flared.

Its eerie blue flame illuminated our bedraggled figures as we danced for joy, gabbling about hot soup, dry shirts, about a great spitting, crackling bonfire six feet high, the first source of warmth and food for two nights and two days. Bogel and I feverishly heaped wood over the stove in the approved woodsman's cone and blew for our lives. Straub shook the flashlight into a dull gleam and vanished into the jungle to get the water. Timo, lying in the mud wrapped in his hammock, encouraged us anxiously: "Keep it going. Keep blowing. It will catch soon."

Keep blowing? We blew ourselves dizzy, first one, then the other, enormous sucking gulps of air, then the rib-aching expulsion, our faces

168

inches from the wet, mossy wood and the sizzling stove. The heavy smoke billowed into Bogel's face and he rolled away gasping. We kept at it relentlessly, blowing till light dots swam in our eyes, choking and crawling around, scrabbling for fuel, eyes and noses streaming.

Himalayan Sherpas have lungs like leather and can blow the wettest wood into fire, they say. Well, by God, we're no slouches either. We'll blow or bloody well bust. We'll set the whole damn jungle afire. We'll get a blaze going that will steam out the mud and slime and transform us from dank-skinned toads to ragged but warm apes, with something hot in our bellies, even if it's only sugar and water. Water? Come on, Paul, crash your way through, man! Get that container and crash back here quick.

By now we had flames licking up the cone of branches and a red-hot heart of twigs within. More wood, for God's sake! Rip it off the trees! Bark, leaf, mold, roots, anything at all. Pile it on and blow, boys, blow!

There was crackling now, the hiss and pop of green plants burning, and through it, far off, a faint call from Straub asking us to shout to guide him in. I glanced at my watch. He'd been out there one-and-a-half hours groping through the jungle. In ninety minutes we had a fire only one-and-a-half feet high. So back to it, Bogel, let's get this bloody thing roaring. Blow your guts out! Frantically we puffed. Soon we'd have our battered, blackened pan bubbling as we stirred our powdered rations into it—stew, soup, tea. First food for forty-eight hours.

Straub burst into the firelight and we turned

leaping to greet him . . . and then froze. We stared at his empty hands.

"There's no water, fellows. The container had fallen from the cache. It's empty."

The trees were rustling. There was a whoosh of wind, a familiar patter on the leaves. In an instant the rain came through to us, spattering our faces, icily sluicing down our necks. The flames guttered out, the embers hissing and dulling, and soon we were enveloped by the wet, black night. We couldn't even see where our fire had been.

II

TO FIND OUR INDIANS

This was our eleventh bivouac in the mud, our eleventh night with our boots on, the same shirts, the same socks, drenched and smeared with the same filth. We had taken off nothing but the skin of our shins and hands. We dragged out our slop-blanket and crawled under it while the rain drummed down.

It kept up all night and we lay shivering, bellies cramped with hunger, waiting miserably for dawn. At its first glimmer we began packing listlessly. Exhaustion and lack of food gave us the lethargic, spiritless look of men at high altitude on a mountain. We would make a move, then stop to take a breath. To get my heavy pack onto my back I had to lie on the ground, pull the straps over my shoulders, roll over so I was underneath it and rise slowly, first to my knees and at last to my feet. We were all reaching the end of our reserves.

After a hard pull through the undergrowth we reached the site of the first night's bivouac at the foot of the wall. Here was the empty water container and in a plastic bag, a camera which had not been needed on the wall. Then, digging farther in the cache, Straub produced two cans of beer! Only Timo had known of them; Bogel and I gaped incredulously. It was like showing a $1,000 bill to a skid-row bum. The doctor had hauled them all the way from Carrao. One of the cans had leaked but we opened the other and passed it around. It was just after 6 A.M. and our stomachs were completely empty. Timo paused as the can reached him and, looking at it doubtfully, said, "It's very early in the morning for this, isn't it?"

We were too beat to hoot at him but finally he took his share as we toasted our success. Soon we were picking our way down the boulder slope, Timo, pale and sick, inching his way down close to me, the others taking their own line below and to the left. Above us the incredible 1,000-foot-high streamers of water vapor blew out from the falls to mingle with the drifting curtains of rain. Far below were the white cascades of the Angel River.

I was thinking of the Indians. We were five days overdue. Had they gone? Had they held out a day or two and then given us up? Could they be leaving at this very moment when we were only a few miles away?

We were almost at the river now and Bogel

found a route down through the shrub-tangled rocks to the edge of it. Farther down was our crossing point, a wide flat ledge over which the river tumbled in a sixty-foot fall. Bogel held me with a rope as I edged across it, the water tearing at my legs. Once over I belayed the others as they crossed in their turn.

Next came the trackless stretch of jungle that we forced through for two hours until we judged we could turn north toward the trail to the Churún River and base. Hitting that trail was a turning point, a psychological milestone. Just stumble on, boys. Get down that bloody track. You might find the Indians living off the jungle. Don't stop to rest; you'll never get on your feet again if you do. Tramp on, fellows, the ground is leveling. There's a lighter shade of green ahead. The jungle is opening out.

We emerged from the final trees in a sort of limping shuffle, our best effort at a run: "*Gabriel, estás ahí, hombre?* Are you there?"

We tottered into the camp clearing at the river's edge, gasping for breath, legs buckling under us. But no one answered my call. There was no dugout. No fire.

The Indians had gone.

III

TO FEAST OR NOT TO FEAST

We shucked off our packs and collapsed on the ground. Nobody said a word. From time to time one of us would move—sprawl face up, roll on his belly, listlessly shift an arm or leg. The river chuckled through the stones. The leaves overhead were sunlit. A chirrupy bird watched us warily for a move. But we weren't going anyplace.

After a while, still lying there, we began to strip off our filthy clothes. Straub and I were first. Then we noticed that Timo and Bogel were having trouble with their boots and socks. Bogel, gritting his teeth and wincing, removed the laces of his boots completely and eased his heels out. But the rest of his feet wouldn't come. There was barely a shred of skin left on the knuckles of his toes. His flesh, socks and canvas boot tops were stuck together with congealed blood. He must have been in that condition for days and had made no complaint. We hadn't known his feet were bothering him at all.

"I'll have to soak my boots off in the river," he said finally.

Timo was in an even worse state. He had four square inches of skin missing from each ankle. He too had kept this to himself. Straub and I peered at our own feet with some interest. Not a mark on them.

Ten minutes later the four of us struggled to our feet on a single impulse. We were starving. I looked at the date on my watch. "It's now the afternoon of the fifteenth," I said. "We haven't eaten since the night of the twelfth. And that's three days and nights of hard going. We've got to eat or somebody is going to end up ill. Let's search through the kit we left here."

Our first find was a large sheet of cardboard

torn from a supply box. It was on top of the pile of kit, weighted down with a stone. Gabriel had scrawled a message in Spanish on it with charcoal in two-inch-high letters and I translated for the others.

"I left today for Camarata to get food. What I brought is finished. Wait for me here until I come. We are leaving your things here. We could not hold out against hunger, so wait for me."

But the date was missing. We thought it over. They could have left days ago and might be on their way back. But the wisest course was to assume the worst: that they had left that very day, in which case it would be four days more before they got back.

I shook out a pack and collected our remaining powdered food. Straub found a tin of spam, a packet of spaghetti and a two-pound carton of sugar cubes in the kit. This last we pounced on and wolfed down. I got out paper and pencil and began to work out how long we could last.

Meantime the others discovered a cigarette lighter that was without fuel but had enough spark to light a butane stove. Also, an extra tank of gas for the stove. At last we could cook and make that fire. With the climb and march behind us, our hunger had begun to gnaw at us. We felt a dull ache in our bellies and every move was an effort. Bogel turned a pack over and looked up anxiously: "I can hardly shift it. We have to eat, fellows."

Timo, tall and lean anyway, looked like a sick white scarecrow. I studied him a moment, put my ragged notebook down and took the pots to

174

the river to wash them. Then I set up the stove, lit it and put a panful of water on.

"What are you going to make?" Timo asked.

"Well, I'll cook half the spaghetti and when it's ready throw in this custard powder. It will make a sort of sweet mess."

"Spaghetti and custard? Good God! And that's all?" said Bogel.

I explained I had sorted the rations and that there was enough for one meal a day for four days. Squatting around the stove, we argued the matter.

"There's nothing more, I tell you. I've worked it out as carefully as I know how."

"But we're so damn weak we should eat extra now and then cut down even further for the other three days. We'll be doing nothing strenuous, after all," said Bogel.

"Well, I don't know," Timo put in. "Suppose the Indians take longer than four days? What do we do then? There's nothing at all in this jungle."

Straub was silent. He seemed to be staring beyond us at some vision of his own. Suddenly he leaned over, grabbed one of the ration packets and ripped it open. "Put this in too," he said hoarsely.

We stared at him.

He snatched at the spaghetti and threw it into the pan: "Put it *all* in!"

He was shouting, slurring his words like a drunk.

"Hey, hold on, Paul."

But the doctor was kneeling upright, scattering the ration packs, tearing open another one.

"Got to eat!" he yelled. "Got to have food! We're all starving!"

The rest of us looked at each other in alarm. I grabbed Straub by the arm: "Paul! What's the matter with you? Drop those packets, man!"

Timo and Bogel jumped to their feet. Straub was shouting, throwing his arms about: "Let's eat it *all*! Everything!"

We lunged to restrain him, shocked and scared. But he stopped us with a grin. He was pointing behind us, laughing. We spun around, and there was the long gray curiara rounding a bend in the river and surging toward us. A wild hoot of greeting echoed through the jungle and we saw four familiar mahogany faces lit with relief.

It was Gabriel and his Indians.

APPENDICES

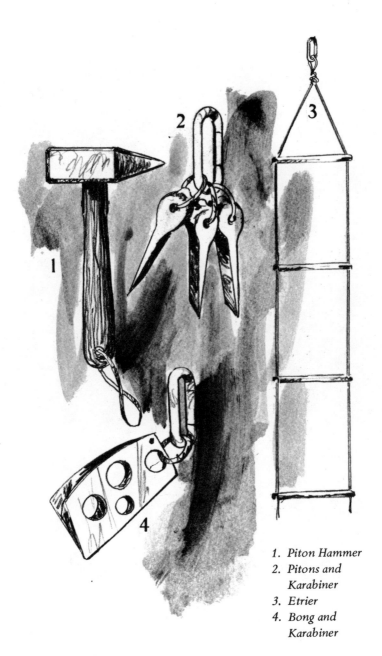

1. Piton Hammer
2. Pitons and
   Karabiner
3. Etrier
4. Bong and
   Karabiner

1 CLIMBING EQUIPMENT

The equipment we used to climb the face of Angel Falls included just about everything you would ever need for difficult rock climbing. But before we get to the list there are a few points to note:

1. Rock climbing is only a branch of its parent sport, mountaineering. On high mountains you have to contend with snow and ice as well as rock. The equipment, skills and training required are correspondingly more complicated. There are far more good rock climbers than good all-around mountaineers. This is mainly due to geography: more people live within striking distance of low mountains with rock routes on them, than on high mountains with snow and ice. But high mountains should be the apprentice rock climber's eventual objective.

2. You don't need any special physical or mental talents for moderate- and middle-standard rock climbing. Anyone in good physical trim can learn to climb at these levels of difficulty. Whether or not you have the qualities needed to advance to the harder routes, only experience will tell. But if you haven't, it doesn't matter. You can climb all your life in glorious situations and never confront a pitch needing *étriers* and bongs, for instance.

3. What you do need from the beginning, however, is a competent friend or professional instructor to teach you. Your progress will be faster and a lot safer. Take one of the training courses listed in the sports magazines.

179

ROPE	We carried three: 120 feet, 150 feet and 200 feet long. For the normal climbing party of two people, one rope, 120 feet long, is usual.
SLINGS	Loops made of odd lengths of rope, three, six, eight feet long or whatever. Their ends may be spliced together or tied, usually with a fisherman's knot. They can be used for running belays, main belays, as a thigh loop for rappeling or hitched over your shoulder to carry karabiners and pitons. Nowadays they are increasingly made of one-inch-wide nylon webbing, which is very strong and easier to handle.
ETRIERS	Five-foot-long ladders made of thin nylon cord with three or four thin alloy strips as steps. Newer types are made of nylon webbing with loops instead of metal strips. You won't need either until you get on really difficult rock. (See Fig. 3)
PITONS	Metal spikes that are driven into the rock for use as belays. There is a hole in the head to which karabiners may be attached. In turn the ropes, slings, *étriers*, foot-loops and other climbing devices may be clipped into the karabiner. Pitons come in all shapes and sizes to fit all types of cracks in the rock (Fig. 1). To use them you need a piton hammer, as shown in the illustration. These weigh about 22 ounces and are normally about 10 inches long. (See Figs. 1 and 2)
KARABINERS	Steel or alloy snaplinks with a spring-loaded gate on one side. They are

180

about 4 in. long and of various shapes. Their uses are too numerous to list. A beginner is first likely to meet them clipped into pitons by his leader as running belays. (*See* Fig. 2 and 4)

BONGS As explained in the text, these metal implements are for use in cracks too wide for pitons. They are an American invention and are replacing wooden wedges used for the same purpose. (*See* Fig. 4)

JUMARS *See* Chapter 5. These devices can be slid up the rope but lock when you apply downward pressure. They are useful when going up fixed ropes and also in more exotic situations, such as when a second man is required to remove pitons on a long, sloping overhang.

CLIFF-HANGERS Slim 4-inch-long hooks that you attach to tiny wrinkles. You can then suspend a foot-loop from them to stand in or use as a handhold. But you need nerves as steely as the hooks.

2 FLIGHT ROUTE FROM CARACAS TO CAMARATA

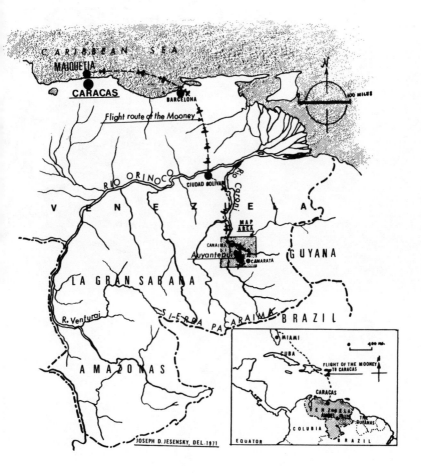

3 A PANORAMIC DIAGRAM OF AUYÁN-TEPUÍ

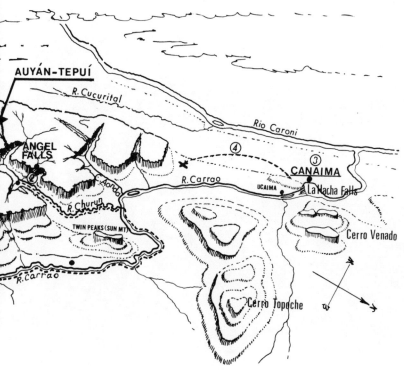

A PANORAMIC DIAGRAM OF AUYÁN-TEPUÍ

Gran Sabana Region - Venezuela - South America

(by Joseph D. Jesensky - 1971)

1. Starting point of boat trip to Angel Falls

2. Site of climb

3. Base camp of Radio Contact Group

4. Aerial Reconnaissance route

-------- River route to Angel Falls

4 TIMO'S ROUTE

Climbs are graded in order of difficulty from I to VI. The numerals correspond more or less to the older system of adjectival grading: Easy, Moderate, Difficult, Very Difficult, Severe, Very Severe (in Britain there is also XS for the super-hard routes).

When a climber has to use pitons (with or without *étriers*) as direct aid, *i.e.,* as holds, the operation is called "artificial" climbing as opposed to "free" climbing. The grading is then A1 to A4.

Rock routes are normally clean and dry, and it is in this state that they are classed. But some gully routes and chimneys are usually slippery and wet, so they are classed in this state.

I am not sure what the normal state of the Timo Route is. When we climbed it, it was in bad condition, plastered with slime. Moreover, it was a first ascent, and things always look worse when you know no one has ever succeeded before you. The following grades are therefore tentative.

There was no grade VI pitch, although Timo's traverse above the Bong Crack was pretty near it. Timo's Chimney, the finger crack in the Labyrinth, the wall up from the chockstone in the Rift, Bogel's Chimney, the wall Timo surmounted via a tree and perhaps Straub's Crack were all grade V. Most of the remaining climbing was III or IV.

The artificial pitches were A1 or A2, except for Bogel's lead over the overhang above Timo's Chimney, which was perhaps A3 because there were no secure cracks for the pitons.

In the French Alps each pitch of a climb is graded and then the climb itself is given an overall standing that takes account of the length of the route, route-finding difficulties, objective dangers such as stone-fall, liability to bad weather, remoteness and other factors. This is an excellent system but not an easy one to transfer from the rock-snow-ice of the Alps to the rock-rain-slime of the Auyán-Tepuí. However, I would say that the Angel is within the next to top grade, or TD (*très difficile*, very difficult).

In other words it is a serious undertaking and for experienced teams only. The rock, although mainly sandstone, is solid. Rotten stretches can generally be avoided and there is little danger of stonefall. However, because there is no frost, it is not generous with cracks for pitons.

The weather is unpredictable. Though we did the climb in the dry season, the unexpected rain penetrated our aluminum match container, which was wrapped in a plastic bag. It got inside the lenses of the 16mm. film camera we carried and ruined all but one of the movie rolls we shot, as well as six rolls of black-and-white stills. After a long dry spell the wall could be climbed in four days. But water would have to be hauled all the way.

We climbed an average of 350 feet a day for the nine days of the ascent (eight-and-a-half days, in fact, because we made one-third of the descent on the afternoon and evening of the ninth day). This was very slow progress for any sort of climbing but was forced on us by slimy rock, time lost on route-finding and hauling heavy packs.

Other climbers had their eye on the face of Angel Falls before our ascent, and maybe they still do. Perhaps the next team will put up a harder and more direct route closer to the falls itself. But a route really close, say, within a couple of hundred feet on either side, is impossible unless the team is prepared to give it maybe six weeks and bolt the whole way on thickly slimed, overhanging rock.

To me, it would be an insane project. But then, that's what people said about our own.

About the Author

David Nott, the author, is a Cambridge law graduate turned newsman. He has worked for *Reuters, United Press International,* the *London Daily Mirror,* the *London Times* and the *Economist.* He is now based in Caracas, Venezuela, as correspondent for several newspapers and part of his routine beat is the Caribbean islands, a circumstance he says he doesn't find overly painful.

Among his achievements he rates highly the ascent, at age twelve, of a cathedral tower in a noted British university town to adjust the clock mechanism so that the bells chimed thirteen times one winter's midnight. He went on to rock climbing at seventeen and reached the top standards of those days in two months "not because I learned the techniques unusually fast," he says, "but because I was an unusually agile monkey. And a lucky monkey at that."

Since then he has climbed throughout Britain, in the Alps, the Andes, and once made two ascents of Kilimanjaro, involving a 140-mile march and 40,000 feet of climbing, in five days. He was a subaltern with a British light infantry regiment in Somaliland at the time and, he explains, "pretty fit." Trained later as an army paratrooper, he took up sport parachuting at age forty-one. On his first jump his chute made a faulty opening and his left leg was fractured in three places. He judges his tensest moment was when, as a ten-year-old during the Blitz, he crawled under the rubble of a destroyed warehouse to mark an "X" in chalk on the fin of an unexploded bomb. "It was the first bet I took of any real consequence," he says.

He now has a share in a yacht with three other beginners. His only voyage so far was all of nine miles long. It took twelve hours beating up Force Eight winds and ended when a heavier gust snapped off four of the mast's six base bolts. With interest in the sea fully aroused by this first outing, he is plotting a solo crossing of "a well-known stretch of water" and wants a sextant for Christmas.

191